REI Editions

All our ebooks can be read on the following devices:
- Computer
- eReader
- iOS
- Android
- Blackberry
- Window
- Tablet
- Mobile phone

Brown Kittel

Macchi M.C. 200 "Saetta"

ISBN 9782372975407

Publication: March 2025

Brown Kittel

Macchi M.C. 200 "Saetta"

REI Editions

Index

Macchi MC 200

The Macchi MC 200 "Saetta", designed by the famous engineer Mario Castoldi , represented a significant evolution in the production of Italian fighter aircraft.
Compared to the Fiat CR 32 and Fiat CR 42 biplanes, which still constituted the backbone of the Italian fighter squadrons at the beginning of the Second World War, the Macchi MC 200, together with its contemporary Fiat G50, was characterised by a low-wing configuration and an entirely metal structure.
The Macchi MC 200 was designed by Mario Castoldi , the designer of the Italian seaplanes participating in the prestigious Schneider Cup , the last of which, the 1933 MC72, broke the speed record for its category with over 700 km/h: this record would not be beaten until 30 years later by a Russian seaplane.
It made its first flight on 24 December 1937 and entered service in 1939: although equipped with a low-powered engine and armed only with a pair of 12.7 mm Breda-SAFAT machine guns, in the latest versions two 7.7 mm Breda-SAFAT machine guns were added to the wings, the Saetta's design was very valid.

- The Macchi MC200 had no particular defects and was equipped with excellent close combat capabilities.

Indeed, its handling was excellent and its stability in high-speed dives exceptional: it could thus duel with the best Allied fighters and emerge undefeated.
Only the Supermarine Spitfire could out-climb it.

On the other hand, the good flight characteristics were offset by low engine power, a barely sufficient horizontal speed and an inadequate armament of only two 12.7 mm machine guns in the fuselage, synchronized for firing through the propeller .

- The cockpit, open, had no heating, and there was no armour to protect the pilot, except in a limited number of examples.

Added to this was the absolute impossibility of performing inverted flight maneuvers due to both the carburetor power supply and, above all, the disengagement of the oil and fuel pumps that such a maneuver would have caused with consequent destruction of the engine; finally, it was an aircraft with an extremely expensive structure to build: approximately 20,000 man-hours, when, for example, 4,500 were enough for the Bf 109E.

From Italy's entry into the war on 10 June 1940 to the armistice of 1943, the Saetta carried out more operational missions than any other Italian aircraft.
Wearing the insignia of the Regia Aeronautica, he operated on almost all fronts of the Second World War, from the Mediterranean Sea to Africa, the Balkans and on the Eastern Front.

An Autonomous Group operated in Russia where it achieved an excellent kill/loss ratio of 88 to 15.

The Macchi MC 200 were built:

- From the parent company Aer.Macchi : 395 examples.
- From Breda, which actually built the largest number: 556 examples.
- From SAI Ambrosini : 223 specimens, in different production batches.

This determined small differences in the painting of the aircraft, both from company to company and from different production series. At a first, immediate examination, it is, however, possible to distinguish the manufacturer of the aircraft by examining the Savoy cross at the tail, since each company adopted a different style for this insignia:

- Breda aircraft were characterised by an equal-armed cross.
- Those produced by Macchi had a longer vertical arm than the horizontal one.
- The planes that came out of the SAI Ambrosini factories bore a cross similar to the Macchi one, but the arms of which extended upwards, downwards and backwards, reaching the edge of the rudder: in the Macchi aircraft, however, they were truncated.

With the Saetta, Italian pilots made that leap in quality from the obsolete canvas and wood biplanes to the more modern monoplanes with very different flight characteristics.

History

After the experience in Spain with the Fiat CR.32 , during the Spanish Civil War, the pilots' request for faster and more modern vehicles was soon accepted by the top brass of the Regia Aeronautica. For this purpose, on 10 February 1936, a specification was issued for the supply of a Land Interceptor Fighter that had to meet the following performances and equipment:

- Maximum speed of 500 km/h.
- Climbed to 6,000 meters in 5 minutes.
- Two hours of battery life.
- Armed with one or two 12.7 mm caliber machine guns.
- Low-wing monoplane wing configuration.
- Adoption of a retractable landing gear.
- Use for propulsion of the Fiat A.74 radial engine.

Three aircraft were presented:
- Macchi MC 200.
- Fiat G.50.
- IMAM RO 51.

The Macchi MC 200 won by a landslide, proving to be the best by far and reporting an overall score of "30", against "25" for the Fiat fighter and "16" for the RO 51.
In the following years, other fighters will be examined by the Royal Air Force: RE 2000, F5, CR42.
Despite this further competition, the C.200 remained the spearhead of the specialty until the entry into service of the Macchi MC 202 in the autumn of 1941.

Its closest competitor, the Reggiane Re.2000, which had good maneuverability at altitude and better low-speed handling, was discarded due to the great vulnerability of its wing fuel tanks and doubts about their structural strength.

Macchi entrusted the project to the engineer Mario Castoldi ; the C.200, sometimes called " Macchi-Castoldi ", hence the acronym MC, was a low-wing monoplane, a type of aircraft of which Eng. Castoldi already had a decade-long experience with his notable racing seaplanes , such as the Macchi M.39, winner of the prestigious Schneider Cup in 1926 and, in 1931, with the very fast MC72, the first to officially bear the acronym MC.

The MC200 with the paint scheme used in North Africa. This example was captured, transferred to the United States and refurbished in 1989. It is currently on display at the National Museum of the United United States Air Force .

Castoldi would have preferred to entrust the propulsion to an inline engine but national engine production was by now oriented almost exclusively towards radial engines, which were also produced under license.

In a short time he managed to build the first prototype, military markings MM336, which was taken into flight for the first time, from the Campo della Promessa in Lonate. Pozzolo , December 24, 1937, piloted by test pilot Giuseppe Burei .

- The machine is beautiful, with graceful lines, with an extremely aerodynamically refined engine cowling , characterised by the "bumps", or those typical undulations, visible at first sight, which enclose the cylinder heads.

The cockpit was closed, in the aircraft of the first production series, by means of a panel sliding backwards: subsequently, in the majority of the examples produced, the cockpit was of the semi-open type, equipped with fold-down side windows on the sides of the fuselage.

First impressions are considered positive but, as successful as it is, it was born with a defect in self-rotation.

Already from the tests carried out on 11 June 1938 in Guidonia , by Major Ugo Borgogno , it resulted that the 90° turn could not be tightened very much because the aircraft tended to tip over to the opposite side, particularly to the right.

- If the turn was closed too much, the Macchi entered a dangerous autorotation: a high-speed stall, due to the detachment of the fluid vein from the constant-profile wing.

It was the same defect that also characterized the contemporary Fiat G.50, IMAM Ro.51, in 1937, and the AUSA AUT 18 and Reggiane Re.2000, in 1939.

In early 1940 two pilots were killed because of this defect.

The cause was the continuous wing profile, which on monoplanes favors the entry into auto-rotation: the Reggiane 2000 and the Caproni Vizzola F5 had a variable wing profile and, therefore, did not incur this phenomenon.

- Deliveries and flights were therefore suspended.

The aircraft was considered, by the average pilot, "unflyable", just as an order for 12 aircraft for Denmark went up in smoke, due to the German invasion.

- Autorotation of an aircraft consists in the phenomenon of detachment of the fluid vein near the ends of the wing panels.

This causes the aircraft itself to rotate around the roll axis, a rotation which, depending on the characteristics of the aircraft involved, can self-extinguish or be galvanized.
This second eventuality can lead to the aircraft becoming uncontrollable, since any attempt to correct the self-rotation motion using the ailerons has the opposite effect of increasing the rotation speed of the aircraft.

- When the wing is stalled and the angle of attack is greater than the stall angle, any increase in the angle of attack causes a drop in the coefficient of climb resulting in a descent of the aircraft.

As the wing descends, the angle of attack increases, causing the coefficient of climb to decrease and the angle of attack to increase.
So reversing the terms: for this reason the angle of attack is unstable when it is greater than the stall angle.
Any change in the angle of attack on one wing will cause the entire wing to rotate, spontaneously and continuously.

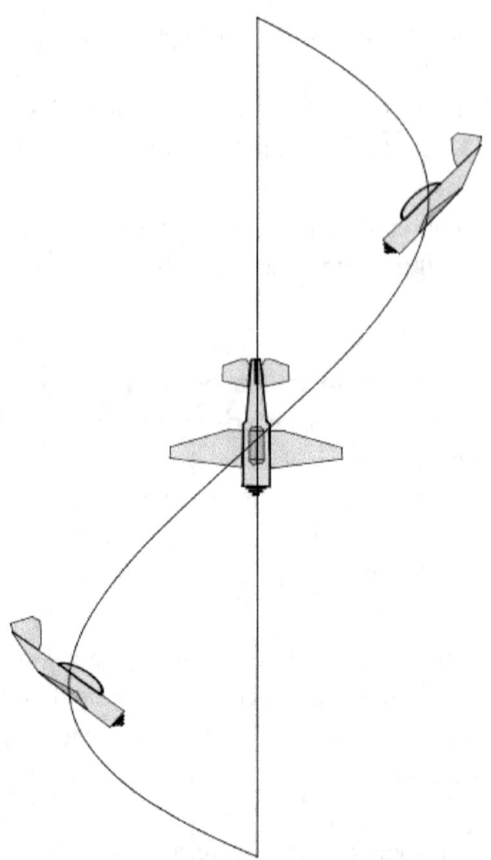

Screw - aggravated stall and auto-rotation

When the angle of attack of an aircraft wing reaches the stall angle, the aircraft is at risk of auto-rotation and may degenerate into a spin, if the pilot does not take corrective action.

Another drawback was the poor rear visibility through the plexiglass of the hood , due to the quality of the plastic laminate and to particular phenomena of light polarization on its surface. Similarly to what was reported for the G.50, the opening of the canopy , above a certain speed, became impossible due to the aerodynamic depression: therefore, the open cockpit solution was proposed again, but this occurred after December 1940, that is, after the first 240 examples.

- The first series of 99 aircraft (MM . 4495-4593), in fact, left the Company, starting from the summer of 1939.

As of November 10, 29 have already been delivered: initially, they flow to the 10th group of the 4th wing, but the aircraft, not well accepted by the pilots of this unit already in the process of transferring to the CR. 42, is transferred to the 6th group of the 1st fighter wing.

In June 1940, the C. 200s were with the 6th group (Catania), with the 152nd (Airasca) and with the 153rd group (Vergiate) of the 54th wing: a total of 144 aircraft.

- Shortly after the beginning of hostilities, two fatal accidents occurred at the 1st Wing, leading to the suspension of flights with this aircraft.

The subsequent investigation allowed to ascertain that it had been the usual, and infamous, phenomena of auto-rotation and, in September, the aircraft was again operational, in the skies of Malta with escorts to the SM. 79s and interception missions.

- The cause of the MC200's troubles was in the wing profile.

Castoldi immediately began experimenting with a new type of wing, but the solution to the self-rotation problem was found by engineer Sergio Stefanutti , chief designer of SAI Ambrosini in Passignano sul Trasimeno.

Based on studies conducted by the German aeronautical engineer Willy Messerschmitt and the American National Advisory Committee on Aeronautics (NACA), the wing section was redesigned according to a variable, rather than constant, profile, obtained by covering parts of the wings with plywood, that is, by gluing layers of balsa plywood to the centre and ends of the wings.

The aircraft now inspires confidence in pilots, has good overall flight quality and aerobatic performance, although it still tends to tip over in very tight right turns, and is virtually vibration-free.

- Thus transformed, the Macchi 200 soon revealed itself to be our best fighter of the time.

Its entry into service on the Greek-Albanian front confirmed it with numerous successes on the Hurricane , but, to save weight, the initial production Macchis had no armour to protect the pilot: armour began to arrive late in the war, sometimes when the units were about to replace the "Saetta" with the brand new Macchi MC202, and, in any case, in limited numbers.

However, once the armor had been fitted, hitting the aircraft was quite laborious and even dangerous.

- In fact, during aerobatic maneuvers, the plane could enter a flat spin, from which the only way out was to parachute, as happened to Leonardo Ferrulli , on July 22, 1941, in Sicily.

The C.200 was in itself an excellent aircraft, but it had a deficit of about 200 hp compared to the British fighters of the period, and was armed with only two 12.7 mm machine guns, while its foreign counterparts were equipped with 8 wing machine guns or a mixed armament of machine guns and 20 mm cannons.

- Over the course of the entire production run, 1,153 examples of the MC 200 were built, including the two prototypes MM .336 and MM .337, built in 24 different batches.

The months of Italian non-belligerence saw an intensification of the efforts of the Italian Consortium for Aeronautical Exports to satisfy the requests of countries that needed airplanes, even if not very modern, before the definitive closure of traditional sources of supply or to better deal with emergencies already underway.

It is enough to recall the case of the CR 42 in Belgium, the Re 2000 in Hungary and the S. 79 in Yugoslavia; even the C. 200 was the object of requests which, however, could not be satisfied due to the lack of political approval or the difficulties in respecting tight delivery deadlines.

The Macchi MC 200 was also presented at the Belgrade Air Show in June 1938 (it was the second MM 337 prototype) and several countries made formal offers such as Sweden, Finland, Romania and Spain.

- Only one formal contract was signed with the Royal Danish Navy which ordered twelve MC 200s in March 1940 to replace the ageing Hawkers. Nimrod .

The events of spring 1940, however, caused the supply to end with the German invasion of the country: Switzerland also requested an offer which the Consortium presented in May 1940 to the Technical Service of the Federal Military Department.

To give an idea of the situations in these uncertain and hectic months, we can say that Switzerland's offer was for 36 complete aircraft, without radios and ammunition, at a unit price of 58,000 dollars, with immediate delivery of 24 units and the subsequent 12 within 3-4 months of the order.

Unlike other aircraft that were being pushed for export, the General Staff was not, however, in favour of selling the C. 200s due to its own pressing needs.

On 1 September 1939, the beginning of the conflict in Europe, the Regia Aeronutica had in charge 29 MC 200s, against 19 G 50s and 143 CR 42s, of which 25 were in the units, while on 10 June 1940, the date of Italy's entry into the war, the C. 200s had risen to 156, of which 103 were in the units, against 118 G 50s and 300 CR 42s.

Among the aircraft in charge of the Experimental Centre there were still the two prototypes:

- The first, MM 336, after having stayed for a long time at Breda as a sample aircraft, returned to Macchi on 23 August 1940: long inactive, it gave its engine to MM 8836 and its airframe returned to Varese in September 1942 where all traces of it were lost.

- The second, MM 337, after an honourable experimental career, where it also served as a sample for camouflage tests, returned to the company and after a thorough overhaul was transported to Rimini in September 1941 by Marshal Spazzoli.

Aside from a few minor modifications, such as the addition of armor to the pilot's seat, sand filters, a new type of radio, and wing spars for small-caliber bombs, the C. 200 remained virtually unchanged throughout its production run.

Worth mentioning is an attempt made by Breda at the beginning of 1942 to increase speed and climbing performance by using the Piaggio P. XIX RC 40 engine with a nominal 1,000 hp.

The installation of the new, bulkier and more massive engine was certainly not a success from the point of view of aerodynamic resistance, so the increase in performance determined in a test cycle in April-May 1942 by test pilot Acerbi was rather disappointing.

Castoldi was very annoyed by the results of a modification that he had not liked from the beginning, and attributed the failure to the actual power of the engine, lower than expected, and to the failure to introduce other modifications he had suggested such as the closed canopy , the retractable tail wheel and the grouping of the oil radiators in the canopy .

Transported to Guidonia , the C. 200 bis MM 8191, disappeared soon and rightly, in the limbo of many disappointing prototypes.

The MC200's best qualities, however, were not its particularly high speed, but its good rate of climb, exceptional maneuverability and structural robustness, which was much appreciated in maneuver combat in later years against more modern and more heavily armed aircraft.

- Its top speed in a dive was also impressive.

During official tests at the Guidonia experimental test center , Bureii reached the remarkable speed of 805 km/h (500 mph) in a dive without any aerodynamic or fluttering problems.

Technique

The Macchi MC200, like its Fiat G.50 counterpart, represented a turning point in Italian aeronautical production of the time, already unsuccessfully undertaken by the Breda Ba.27, that of the adoption of a monoplane wing configuration and an entirely metal structure.

The fuselage was set on a shell structure with four duralumin spars joined by frames in stamped duralumin segments; the covering was in stamped superavional , nailed to the structure with totally embedded riveting , so as to constitute a surface with the least aerodynamic resistance.

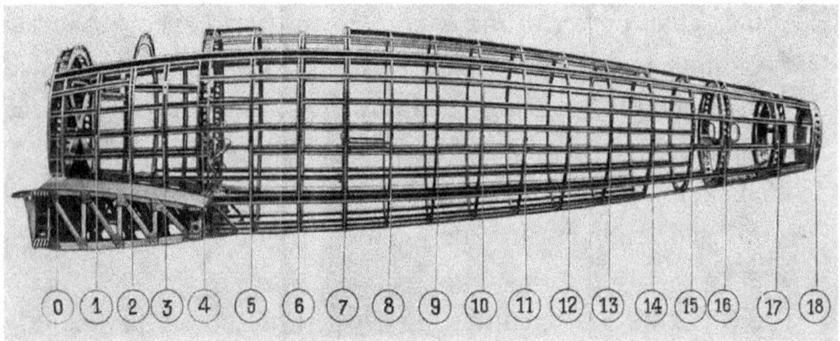

Fuselage - Longitudinal view

The main fuel tank, with a capacity of 241 litres, was placed between the two side members of the central part, while the upper part housed the weapons, ammunition boxes and spent case boxes.

- This was a characteristic of the Italian fighters of the time: they did not want to waste the precious metal material after the weapons were fired, accepting the penalty of useless weight after the fight.

Two opening hatches in the upper fuselage allowed for weapons maintenance.

Already in the first versions with a closed cockpit by a sliding roof and in the subsequent ones with an open cockpit, a special resistant anti-rollover structure was built into the rear fairing of the cockpit.

- The front and rear parts of the windshield were fixed, while the central part was mobile and allowed for parachute launching if necessary.

The tanks for the fire extinguisher, the oxygen system and the start-up system were located immediately behind the cockpit, while a second fuel tank, with a capacity of 150 litres, was located under the floor of the cockpit and was connected to the main one with a flexible hose.

- All tanks were armored, being able to withstand gun holes up to 12.7 mm caliber.

Under the fuselage there were connections for an additional external tank, with a capacity of 77 litres, which was used extremely rarely: the pilot's position was quite elevated, which allowed him excellent visibility.

In the first series a folding roof was adopted, which however was found to present the problem of the impossibility of opening beyond a certain speed due to the pressurization: furthermore, fewer problems arose due to the opacification of the transparent material of the rear part, for which reason in the subsequent series the semi-open version was chosen.

The rear ended in a classic single fin tailplane with cantilevered horizontal planes.

The empennage consisted of a fixed horizontal plane and a fixed vertical plane followed by the elevator and steering rudders respectively: the spars of the fixed plane and the fin were made of high-strength steel tube, the ribs and the covering were made of duraluminium.

The shaft tube of the rudders and steering rudders was made of steel, the ribs and surrounds were made of duralumin, the covering of canvas.

The fixed plane was adjustable in flight, the rear spar was fixed with supports to the fuselage and these supports allowed the plane itself to rotate by a few degrees.

The front spar, on the other hand, was fixed to a mobile support which, by means of a screw system, could be raised by 1° 45' and lowered by 5° 30' and was controlled by a mechanical device located to the right of the pilot.

The landing gear was retractable during flight; it consisted of two identical and distinct half-carriages located in the wings. Each one consisted of a fork with an oleo-pneumatic shock absorber stem , a fork that carried a FAST type wheel equipped with brakes with Pirelli 600x216x200 tyres.

Each shock absorber shank was connected to a horizontal axis that rotated in special bushings fixed in the wing spars: these semi-trolleys were each operated by a hydraulic jack that rotated the shank towards the inside of the aircraft and made it disappear into the leading edge of the wings and into the central part of the fuselage in special compartments, which in turn were closed by doors partly fixed to the shock absorber shank and partly to the fuselage. The tail wheel could also be hidden during flight and was composed of an oleo-pneumatic shock absorber shank with a wheel fitted with a SPIGA 260 x 80 type tyre.

The trolley was equipped with a double FAST type compressed air brake applied to the wheel drums.

- This air was contained in a cylinder equipped with a loading valve and was the same cylinder that was used to start the engine.

From the cylinder, a pipe went to a reduction valve: before the valve, a socket was provided for the pressure gauge indicating the air pressure in the cylinder itself.

The wing was a monoplane with a thick, biconvex profile, with thickness and depth decreasing towards the extreme edge.

- It was divided into three parts, a central one and two lateral ones that were easily removable. The construction was entirely made of metal.

Two stringers with superavional soles and nailed sides in superavional sheet , suitably drilled, and stiffened with internal frames corresponding to the ribs and diagonally.

The connecting rods fixed to the ends of the side members were high-strength steel hinges with pins having a taper of 2.255 on the diameter.

The ribs, in the central part between the two side members, were built with duralumin profiles connected to each other with riveted plates: the first two ribs were special, being wider and more robust than the others.

- The leading edge of the wing was removable from the landing gear to the tip, and was fixed to the forward spar with screws.

Its construction was similar to the rest, i.e. duraluminium ribs with superavional covering : the rotation axis of the trolley was located on the two side members.

This axle was then mounted on the wing while the lifting jack was part of the fuselage centre plane.

The leading edge, from the wing tips to the landing gear rotation axis, carried the compartments for concealing the latter.

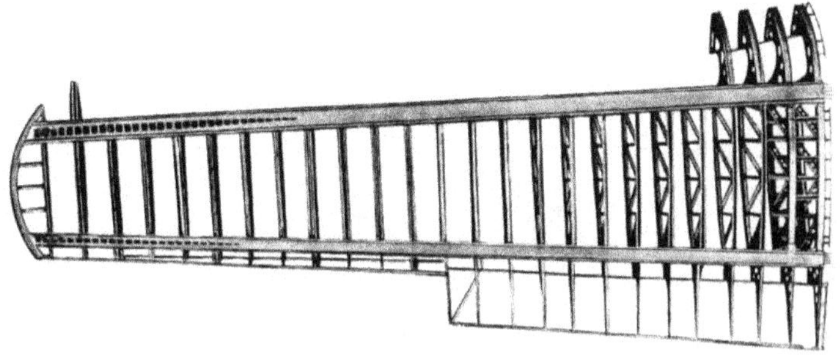

- The wings were equipped with flaps, which ran from the fuselage to about halfway up the wing and from there to the wingtips where the ailerons were located.

The ailerons were constructed entirely of metal, with duralumin profile ribs connected to each other, as in the wing ribs, by riveted plates.
The spar was made of tube divided into three parts connected with steel joints, and the hinges were made of steel with ball bearings.

- The cover was made of canvas.

The wing flaps were also made of metal, with duraluminium ribs and surrounds, steel tube side members, and the cover was made of superaviònal .
The ailerons and tailplane controls were all by means of tubes, eliminating cables and the associated need for adjustment.
The control of the flaps was independent of that of the ailerons and was connected to the hydraulic circuit of the landing gear.

- The maximum depression of the high lift flaps was 45°.

The Piaggio propeller pitch control was installed from the 25th aircraft onwards, since up to the 24th aircraft the ethics were Fiat type with constant speed: the control was electric.

- To reduce the effect of the propeller reaction torque, the left wing half had a larger span than the right wing half (170 mm); although they had the same surface area, the wings obviously had a different chord at the end.

The feature was certainly not the best in terms of aerodynamics, but Castoldi retained it also in the subsequent MC 202 and MC 205.

Access to the cockpit was easy, with no exhaust fumes, the seat was comfortable and adjustable, but only by specialist ground staff: the controls were convenient and rationally arranged, including the extra power (+100 rpm).

The flaps required 46 hand pumps, rather uncomfortable (a control like in the G.50 would have been preferable), the brakes were also good, the landing gear was rather slow and could be operated with less rational controls than the mediocre Ro.51.

- The aircraft was capable of taking off without yaw, improving the clearance with the flaps at 15 degrees.

Propulsion was entrusted to a Fiat A.74 RC .3 8 engine, a 14-cylinder double-star air-cooled radial, capable of delivering a power of 870 hp (618 kW) at 2,520 rpm at take-off and 740 hp at sea level, combined with a three-bladed metal propeller with variable pitch in flight.

- 87 octane petrol.

Unlike the G.50, which adopted the same engine, a textured cowling was used in correspondence with the rocker arms located at the apex of the individual heads, thus significantly reducing the frontal bulk and also improving visibility.

The oil tank was located in the engine mount and had a capacity of 42 litres: in turn, the oil radiator was located on the front external surface of the engine hood.

The armament consisted of two 12.7 mm Breda- SAFAT machine guns, one right-handed and one left-handed, complete with cylinders for pneumatic rearming. They were arranged at the front, fixed and parallel to the aircraft's centreline , and fixed on longitudinal supports adjustable in height and laterally, which were attached to frame no. 0 and to the rear of the fuselage.

- Each of these supports carried a double-acting adjustable spring shock absorber to absorb the shock of the shot.

Their direct shot passed through the propeller just above the engine cowling.

In the center, between the two guns, were placed the two cassettes with a maximum capacity of 370 rounds each, starting from the 13th aircraft; for the first 12 aircraft the maximum capacity was 310 rounds each.

After the 25th aircraft, the machine guns were equipped with a flame arrester so as not to blind the pilot when firing.

- In the fighter-bomber version, the MC 200 CB, there were auxiliary attachments under the wings for two bombs of up to 160 kg each or for two auxiliary tanks of 150 litres each.

At the date of the armistice, 52 examples were in service, 33 of which were still efficient.

The Macchi C 200 was already equipped with all the necessary instruments: the cockpit contained a variometer, altimeter, anemometer, gyro-directional instrument and magnetic compass.

Also in the cockpit was the centering system which was placed in the center of the instrumentation.

- Aerodynamic purists objected to the apparent "hump" on the fuselage which was, instead, a carefully studied solution to give the pilot maximum visibility, exceeding the requirements of the competition specification, without penalising aerodynamic resistance.

The fact that it was the result of careful planning was demonstrated a few years later by the prototype of the C 201 which achieved the same performances with the same A.74 engine, without the "hump" and an airframe equivalent to the C 200.

Alongside the prototype, which was assigned the military serial number MM 336, a non-flying cell was built for static tests and a second example designated MM 337 which would fly a few months later, in May 1938.

Macchi MC 200 Saetta preserved at the National Museum of the United United States Air Force

- The production aircraft did not differ much from the two prototypes.

In addition to minor modifications, the major modifications that were agreed with the technical bodies of the Ministry and which were introduced, where possible, already on the aircraft of the first series, were:

- The release of the aileron control system making them independent from the flaps : Castoldi 's project envisaged the partial lowering of the ailerons with the lowering of the flaps .
- The elimination of the tail gear retraction system which was made fixed.
- The introduction of static and dynamic compensation on the rudder.
- The introduction of the open cabin.
- The modification of the wing's leading edge, which was originally fixed to the front spar by means of lag screws, was replaced, very wisely, by special screws with olives:

the leading edge complex was, in fact, made integral with the , using a total of 604 screws of three different types.

Finally, the original Fiat-Hamilton propeller was replaced by a Piaggio propeller, also with variable pitch and constant revolutions, whose blades had been traced directly by Castoldi himself .

Technical features

Dimensions and weights

- Length: 8.19 meters
- Wingspan: 10.58 meters
- Height: 3.51 meters
- Wing area: 16.81 m ^{2}
- Wing loading: 142.2 km/m ^{2}
- Empty weight: 1,960 kg
- Load weight: 2,390 kg
- Specimens: 1,153

Propulsion

- Engine: one Fiat A.74 RC .3 8 radial
- Power: 870 hp (618 kW)

Performance

- Maximum speed: 503 km/h at 4,500 meters
- Stall speed: 128 km/h
- Climbing speed:
  - ✓ at 1,000 meters in 1' and 3"
  - ✓ at 2,000 meters in 2' and 10"
  - ✓ at 3,000 meters in 3' and 24 "
  - ✓ at 4,000 meters in 4' and 35"
  - ✓ at 5,000 meters in 5' and 52"
  - ✓ at 6,000 meters in 7' and 33"
- Take-off run: 260 meters
- Landing run: 300 meters

- Range: 570 km or 870 km with two auxiliary tanks
- Tangency: 8,900 meters.

Armament

- Machine guns: 2 x 12.7 mm Breda/SAFAT in the fuselage, synchronized and firing through the propeller disc with 370 rounds per gun.

Versions

- **Prototype**

Two prototypes, MM .336 and MM .337, with Fiat A.74 RC .3 8 engine, closed cockpit, fully retractable landing gear and tail wheel.
First flight on December 24, 1937 in the hands of test pilot Giuseppe Burei .

- **Macchi MC 200**

First mass-produced version, equipped with a modified wing profile and a Fiat A.74 RC .3 8 engine.
Starting from the 241st example, the fully enclosed cabin was abandoned and, after the first 146 examples, the retractable tail wheel.

- **Macchi MC 200 A2**

Factory designation for aircraft powered by the Fiat A.74 RC .3 8 engine, fitted with the wings and landing gear of the Macchi MC202.

- **Macchi MC 200 AS**

Designation of units intended for use in Italian North Africa (ASI), they are equipped with a sand filter on the carburetor air intake.

- **Macchi MC 200 B2**

Factory designation for aircraft powered by the Fiat A.74 RC .3 8 engine, fitted only with the wing leading edge of the Macchi MC 202.

- **Macchi MC 200 Bis**

Factory designation of the MM .8191 model, built by Breda and equipped with a 1,180 hp Piaggio P. XIX engine.
First flight in April 1942, equipped with a more powerful engine and a larger propeller, it reached 535 km/h, but remained at the prototype stage.

- **Macchi MC 200 CB**

Aircraft intended for the Italian North Africa (ASI) theatre of operations, converted into a fighter-bomber.
They mounted two 3 kg bomb carriers, each of which could carry a 50, 100 or 160 kg bomb.

- **Macchi MC 201**

RC.4 0 engine , the aircraft featured some aerodynamic improvements, such as the fuselage without the dorsal bulge and the closed cockpit.
Since the planned engine was not yet available, the prototype was equipped with the 840 hp Fiat A.74 RC .3 8 and was flown in August 1940 by test pilot Guido Carestiato, reaching a speed of 512 km/h.

Technical features:

- Engine: Fiat A.76 RC.4 0 , 1,000 kp air-cooled radial .
- Wingspan: 10.58 meters.
- Length: 8.45 meters.
- Height: 3.51 meters.
- Wing area: 16.80 m² .
- Empty weight: 2,030 kg.
- Takeoff weight: 2,466 kg.
- Maximum speed: 525 km/h
- Autonomy: 800 km.
- Tangency: 9,000 meters.
- Armament: Two 12.7 mm machine guns in the fuselage.

The aircraft had no follow-up since the planned engine, the Fiat A.76, was approved only in mid-1943.

Prototype of the Macchi MC 201.

Breda-SAFAT machine guns

The 7.7 mm and 12.7 mm Breda-SAFAT machine guns were the weapons most used by the Regia Aeronautica during the Second World War: they were born from the collaboration of the Società Italiana Ernesto Breda per Costruzioni Meccaniche and the Società Anonima Fabbrica Armi Torino (SAFAT).

The birth of these weapons was due to the desire of the Regia Aeronautica to have better machine guns to face the new generations of enemy aircraft, characterized by superior performance and better armament.

Breda based its design on the drawings of the Browning M2 machine gun, adapting it to Italian needs, in particular in the change of cartridge from the Allied calibres 7.62×63 mm and 12.7×99 mm to the Italian standard calibres 7.7×56 mm R and 12.7 mm $\times$ 81 mm SR.

- The latter, in particular, however, weakened the weapon and the goal of a lighter machine gun with a high rate of fire was not achieved.

In any case, the Breda/Browning weapon participated in the competition against similar projects made by the much more powerful industrial group Fiat, which proposed new weapons designed by its subsidiary SAFAT (Società Anonima Fabbricazione Armi Torino). But the Breda/Browning, in its two versions, proved superior, especially in terms of weight, which was 5 kg less than the Fiat-SAFAT project .

Despite pressure from Fiat, the Royal Air Force awarded the supply contract to Breda.

Having rejected its appeal in court and ordered to pay the legal costs, Fiat temporarily withdrew from the small arms sector, even selling SAFAT to the same Società Italiana Ernesto Breda per Costruzioni Meccaniche, which became the undisputed leader in the sector in Italy.

The Breda-SAFATs armed almost all Italian fighters and bombers of that period: the Fiat CR.42 , Fiat G.50, Macchi MC 200, Macchi MC 202 and Reggiane Re.2000 fighters were armed with two Breda 12.7 mm machine guns and, in the later examples, two Breda 7.7 mm wing-mounted machine guns.

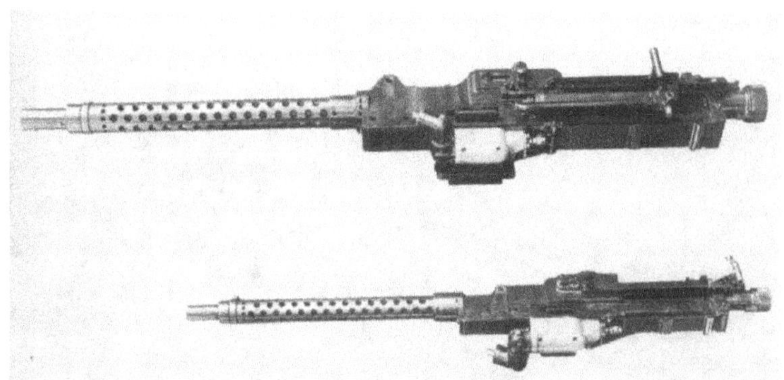

The 7.7 mm and 12.7 mm Breda-SAFAT machine guns

This armament proved inadequate in the first years of the war and so the German 20 mm Mauser MG 151/20 cannon was adopted, installed in up to 3 pieces on the new Macchi MC205, Fiat G.55 and Reggiane Re.2005 fighters, in addition to the two usual 12.7 mm guns firing through the propeller disc.

After the war, the 7.7 mm Breda-SAFAT , in the field version, remained in service with the VAM of the Italian Air Force until the 1980s.

The operation was recoil-operated, with a short barrel recoil, and the bolt unlocked by the Mascarucci lever mechanism : the firing cycle was with the bolt closed.

- Cooling was by air, through the perforated barrel cover.

The feeding, by belt in the aeronautical systems or by 150-round cassette magazines in the field version, was reversible, from the right or from the left.

On fighters, the machine gun was often used in a twin installation, fixed "in fighter" on the engine cowling , firing through the propeller disk: in this installation the rate of fire dropped to 575 rounds/minute.

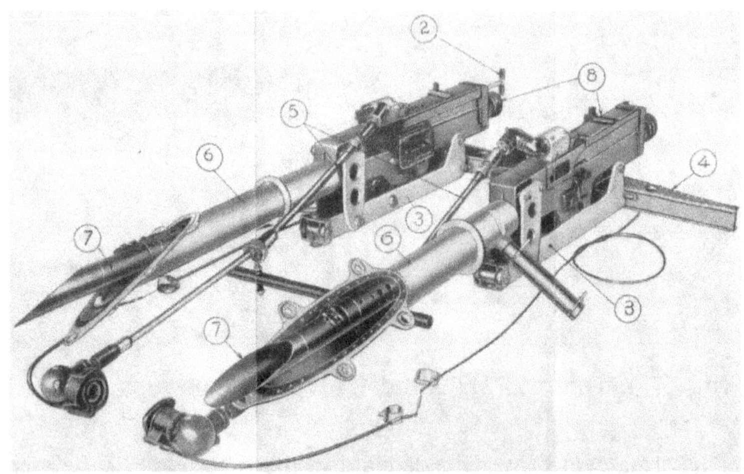

On bombers and transport aircraft, the Breda-SAFATs constituted the standard defensive armament, installed on a single rotating Type A2 turret as on the CANT Z.501, on a manual Type D twin turret, the remote-controlled Type E and Type Z twin turrets, the retractable ventral Type G9 and on many others.

For field use, both versions had both stanchion mounts for anti-aircraft fire and tripods for use as a support gun for infantry.

- It was also installed as an anti-aircraft weapon on some MAS.

A feature of the 7.7 mm version was the ability to also use the similar .303 British ammunition of British production.

Instead, the explosive/incendiary/tracer (HEIT) rounds were domestically produced, loaded with 0.8 grams of Pentrite and were considered very effective.

The normal sequence inside the tapes was as follows: 2 × ball, 1 × tracer, 1 × armor-piercing, 1 × explosive.

However, its slow rate of fire and low muzzle velocity made it ineffective at long ranges, while the intrinsic limitations of the 12.7 mm × 81 mm calibre were fully demonstrated during the first two years of the war, so much so that it was replaced on new production aircraft with a 20 mm cannon-machine gun.

The muzzle velocity of the 12.7 mm × 81 mm SR Breda cartridge was lower than that of the equivalent .50 BMG cartridge since the ammunition was 12.7 × 81 mm rather than 12.7 × 99 or 12.7 × 108 mm.

- The firing energy of the Breda, in fact, is only 10,000 joules compared to the 16,000-17,000 joules of other cartridges.

Thus, while the Breda-SAFATs were reliable weapons, they had the worst power-to-weight ratio of all contemporary machine guns mounted on World War II aircraft.

In comparison, the Japanese Ho-103 used the same license-produced 12.7×81mm ammunition, but was 6–7 kg lighter and had a rate of fire of 800–900 rounds per minute, at least 20% higher.

Not even Alfredo Scotti of Isotta Fraschini , who tried to lighten and improve the performance of the Breda with his Scotti/Isotta Fraschini model , could match its rate of fire or reliability.

- Although the 12.7 mm shell had low destructive capacity with only 0.8 grams of explosive and despite the availability of larger caliber high explosive ammunition, Italian pilots appreciated the capabilities of this cartridge in the armor-piercing incendiary version.

Nearly all countries had adopted the 12.7-13.2 mm explosive cartridge, but had come to the conclusion that this ammunition was too weak and ineffective against armour to justify its cost, so they turned to weapons in a calibre of 20 mm or larger.

- The 12.7mm×81mm SR was an Italian machine gun cartridge used from the Ethiopian War in 1935 throughout World War II.

This ammunition was derived from the English .50 Vickers 0.5 inch, 12.7 × 81 mm metric round, which had been produced by Vickers since 1921.

This cartridge did not attract particular interest from the British armed forces, but did arouse the interest of Italy and Japan.

The ammunition produced by the Società Italiana Ernesto Breda per Costruzioni Meccaniche derives in particular from the export version produced in 1923 by Vickers called .5 V/565, obtained by modifying the base from Rimless to Semi-Rimmed and therefore called 12.7 mm × 81 mm SR.

It was adopted by Italy in 1935 with the Breda-SAFAT and Scotti/Isotta Fraschini machine guns , which armed most of the aircraft of the Regia Aeronautica from the Ethiopian War to the Second World War.

It remained in production until the 1980s, when the last Breda-SAFAT field version of the Italian Air Force were decommissioned.

Since the SAFAT armed the aircraft of the Corpo Truppe Volontarie and the Fiat CR.32 fighters , supplied to the Nationalists during the Spanish Civil War, the cartridge was produced in Spain by the "Pirotécnica" company of Seville.

Hungary produced the Reggiane Re.2000 under license, in two models Heja (falcon in Hungarian) I and II and this fighter was armed with the Gebauer GKM Machine gun. Gun 1940.M, which used the 12.7 Breda.

In 1941 it was adopted by the Imperial Japanese Army for the Ho-103 Type 1 machine guns.

It was produced with various types of projectiles:

- Jacketed bullet: lead core jacketed in aluminum: weighed approximately 34.5 grams.
- Armor-piercing: The projectile consists of a copper jacket covering a core of high hardness and density.
- Armor-piercing-incendiary : the jacket , in the ogive part, has four small holes that communicate with a cavity present between the tip and the armor-piercing projectile, loaded with white phosphorus: it was recognizable by the blue painted tip.
- Tracer: in the rear part of the nose cone there is a cavity containing a small pyrotechnic charge which, burning during flight, leaves a trail of different colors, allowing the adjustment of the shot: they are recognizable by the red painted tip.
- Armor-piercing-incendiary-tracer : combines the various characteristics in the same projectile.
- Incendiary-Tracer : combines the two characteristics.
- High explosive : the warhead contained a firing pin that activated a charge of 0.8 grams of pentyrite and exploded on contact with the target: it was recognizable by the yellow painted base of the warhead.

Other countries had also developed explosive projectiles, but the Italians were the first to produce this technology on such small-caliber ammunition, or rather, the other nations gave up on building explosive ammunition of such a small caliber, believing that they would have a power decidedly inferior to the 20 mm caliber, preferred by France and Germany, and the Japanese navy, later adopted also by the United Kingdom and, therefore, made almost universal, or to the 23 mm, typically Soviet.

So, they decided not to undertake research that they considered a waste of money: even the USA, which was massively using 12.7 caliber weapons, albeit with much heavier projectiles, considered it useless to arm them with explosive projectiles.

Fiat A.74 RC .3 8 Engine

The Fiat A.74 RC .3 8 Ciclone was a 14-cylinder double-star air-cooled radial aircraft engine, produced by the Italian company Fiat Aviazione in the 1930s and mounted on numerous aircraft of the Regia Aeronautica during the Second World War, including the Macchi MC 200 "Saetta" fighter monoplanes, the Fiat G.50 and the Fiat CR.42 biplane .

- Powered by a single-body Zenith carburetor with pressure limiter and fuel mixture preheating.

The engine was designed by FIAT in the mid-1930s, based on the similar American Pratt & Whitney R1535 engine and according to the directives of the General Staff of the Royal Air Force aimed at favouring the construction of air-cooled engines.

- There were, however, numerous design differences between the two engines, including the bore and stroke measurements, and construction.

These were due both to the need to simplify production and to the need to use autarchic materials: furthermore, the A.74 was characterised by the adoption of a centrifugal compressor optimised for 3,800 metres of altitude and by the transmission of motion to the propeller interposed by a speed reducer.

- Compared to the Pratt & Whitney R1535, FIAT introduced various distinctive modifications and produced the A.74 until the early 1940s, with a total of approximately 5,500 units, including those built under license by Officine Meccaniche Reggiane.

In order to simplify production and the logistical management of supplies and maintenance, the A.74 adopted the same bore as the larger A.80 engine, so as to be able to use various identical and interchangeable components, including cylinders, pistons and valves.

The A.74, like the A.80, had the following construction characteristics:

- Supercharging by means of a centrifugal compressor mechanically driven by the engine, optimised for altitudes of 3,800 metres.
- Epicyclic speed reducer with bevel gears (Farman type) for transmitting motion to the propeller.
- Exhaust valves internally cooled with sodium salts.
- Cylinder cooling fins, patented by FIAT.
- Three-part light alloy base.

Furthermore, the crankshaft was made up of two pieces and had three main bearings: the central one was formed by a large diameter disc-shaped element, onto which two discs were bolted, integral with the connecting rod pins of the two stars and which constituted the internal ring of a cylindrical roller bearing.

Power:

- 870 hp (648 kW) at 2,500 rpm at take-off.
- 740 hp (544 kW), normal ground power.
- 840 hp (618 kW), homologated power at 2,400 rpm at 3,800 meters and 1.00 Bar pressure provided by the compressor.
- 960 hp (715 kW), at 3,000 meters maximum.

The FIAT A.74 represented a turning point in the production of aircraft engines by the Italian company, which until then had focused on liquid-cooled V12 engines, becoming the forerunner of a series of developments aimed at producing engines with ever greater displacement and power, albeit less successful, such as the A.76, A.80 and A.82.

The FIAT A.74 was built in various versions, with different adjustments and operating characteristics, and was used mainly on fighter aircraft and fighter-bombers during the Second World War. Although it remained in use even when its performance was already surpassed, especially on front-line fighters, it demonstrated excellent reliability and ease of maintenance, even in critical operational contexts that required the use of low-quality fuels and in extreme climates, such as the Libyan desert or the Russian winter.

Despite mass production and the export of several examples abroad, the A.74 was a rather rare engine due to the various losses and the progressive decommissioning during the second part of the war.

The Museum's specimen has been dissected for educational purposes and allows for a detailed illustration of all its main construction features.

In addition to the RC .3 8 version, a smaller number of the RC .4 2 version was produced, with a power recovery altitude of 770 hp at 4,200 metres, mainly used on the Fiat G.12 transport aircraft and on the models intended for training the Macchi MC 200 fighter.

Characteristics techniques

- Manufacturer: FIAT Aviazione, Turin, from 1935 until the early 1940s.
- Designer: Tranquillo Zerbi and Antonio Fessia
- Description: 14-cylinder double-star aircraft engine, aluminum crankcase with three main bearings: steel cylinders with hot-screwed light alloy heads, hemispherical combustion chambers, light alloy pistons, main connecting rod and H-shaped connecting rods , two-part crankshaft connected by bolts.
- Bore: 140 mm
- Stroke: 145mm
- Displacement: 31250 cm³
- Compression ratio: 6.70:1
- Length: 1,045 mm
- Diameter: 1,200 mm
- Power: 870 hp (648 kW) at 2,500 rpm at take-off
- Specific consumption: 270 g/hp/h
- Specific power: 26.9 hp/l
- Distribution: 2 overhead valves per cylinder controlled by rods and rocker arms, exhaust valves internally cooled with sodium salts.
- Fuel system: petrol, with a single-body Zenith-Stromberg carburetor , placed upstream of the compressor and equipped with a pressure limiter and preheating of the fuel mixture.
- Supercharging system: Mechanically driven centrifugal compressor with straight-tooth gears, elastic coupling and 8.78:1 multiplication ratio , adaptation altitude 3,800 metres.

- Ignition system: two spark plugs per cylinder powered by two independent Marelli distributor magnets
- Cooling system: air
- Lubrication system: forced, with gear pumps.
- Starting system: pneumatic with a 12 litre cylinder at 15 bar (for 2 starts) and with a Garelli compressor for recharging.
- Empty weight: 590 kg
- Mass/power ratio: 0.70 kg/hp
- Propeller reduction ratio: 0.725:1 with Farman type bevel gear epicyclic reduction gear : the standard RC 38 version has a propeller reduction ratio of 0.655:1.

On-board instruments

The instruments installed on board the aircraft are:

In the center:

1. compass
2. turn indicators
3. 8,000 meter altimeter
4. Speedometer from km/h 560
5. variometer

Left:

6. windshield opening command
7. compressor pressure gauge
8. 3,000 rpm rev counter
9. oil telethermometer
10. brake fin
11. telepyrometer
12. telepyrometer switch
13. siren switch
14. spy
15. 15 atmosphere oil pressure gauge
16. petrol pressure gauge

To the right:

17. 2nd speed indicator from km/h 560
18. Allemano type trolley pump pressure gauge 250 atmospheres
19. Allemano type 80 atmosphere tail wheel accumulator pressure gauge
20. Machine gun rearm
21. Knook-Out » type fire alarm
22. electrical and mechanical indicator, landing gear and tail wheel
23. trolley circuit breaker
24. spy
25. 10 atmosphere Fast type trolley brake pressure gauge, Allemano construction .
26. clock.

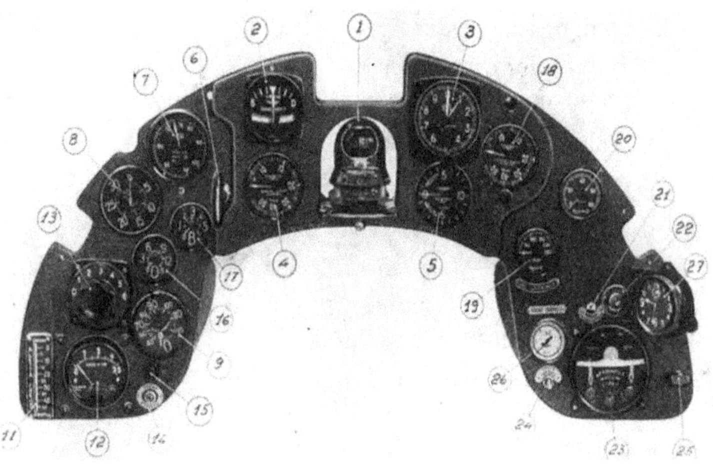

Versions

- **Prototypes**

Two prototypes (MM.336 and MM.337) with Fiat A.74 RC.3
8 engine , closed cockpit, fully retractable landing gear and tail
wheel.
First flight on December 24, 1937 in the hands of test pilot
Giuseppe Burei .

- **MC 200**

First mass-produced version, equipped with a modified wing
profile and Fiat A.74 RC .3 8 engine.
Starting from the 241st example, the fully enclosed cabin was
abandoned and, after the first 146 examples, the retractable tail
wheel.

- **MC 200 A2**

Factory designation of the version with Fiat A.74 RC .3 8
engine, and wing and undercarriage of the C.202.

- **MC 200 B2**

Factory designation of the version with Fiat A.74 RC .3 8
engine, and only the wing leading edge of the C.202.

- **MC 200 AS**

Version obtained by converting the specimens intended for the Italian North Africa (ASI) theatre of operations.

It had a sand filter fitted to the carburetor air intake.

After the end of the war, this Macchi was used for training tasks in Lecce until 1947. Once decommissioned, it was given to the institute as a training cell in the Aeronautical Construction section: unfortunately, here the aircraft lost its original livery replaced by a red one with false cockades and inverted colors. It remained at this site until 1962, when, fortunately, it was recovered by the Air Force and transferred to the Historic Aircraft Collection Center in Vigna di Valle.

- **MC 200 CB**

ASI) theatre of operations, destined for the fighter-bomber role.

They mounted two wing bomb carriers weighing 3 kg and capable of carrying a 50, 100 or 160 kg bomb.

- **MC 200 Bis**

Factory designation for an example built by Breda, on the airframe of example MM.8191 , equipped with a Piaggio P.XIX RC45 Piaggio engine capable of 1,180 hp (880 kW) at 4,500 metres (14,800 ft).

First flight on 11 April 1942 from Milan-Bresso piloted by Luigi Acerbi.

The aircraft was then fitted with a larger propeller and a revised engine cowling. The maximum speed in the studies was 535 km/h.

It did not enter production as the C.200 as it was replaced by more advanced models.

- **MC 201**

Previously to the C.200 Bis, an MC200 (MM . 436) had flown with a revised fuselage and an 870 hp Isotta Fraschini-Astro A.140RC.40 engine .
It was then equipped with a Fiat A.74 RC.3 8 engine of 840 hp, in place of the unavailable Fiat A.76 RC.4 0 of 1,000 hp .

Macchi MC 201

The C.201 prototype flew for the first time in August 1940 in the hands of test pilot Guido Carestiato , reaching a speed of 512 km/h, compared to the 505 km/h average achieved by the production examples.

- The aircraft, in fact, benefited from aerodynamic improvements such as the fuselage without the humpback bulge and the closed cockpit.

The efforts dedicated to the MC201 project were reduced to the bare minimum, modifying the design of the C.200 fuselage to adapt it to the new Fiat A.76 engine: the C.201 was built in only two examples which received the serial numbers MM 436 and MM 437. The two aircraft never made it to flight with the long-awaited Fiat A.76 engine and, only for the sake of contractual commitment, they were completed with the A.74, the standard engine of the C.200, while enthusiasm for the more valid MC202 was fervent.

The first flight of the C.201 was performed by Carestiato on 25 August 1941, one year after the C.202, and the second in the following September.

The two aircraft were then set aside and, after the resolution of a dispute with the Air Force Administration for the recognition of the additional costs compared to the original contract, they received the serial numbers MM 8616 (ex 436) and MM 8617 (ex 437) and were transported to Guidonia by Marshal Gori and Sergeant Staube on 28 June 1942.

Use

The first MC 200s were ready in the spring of 1939 and were delivered to the Regia Aeronautica in the same year.

By 1 September 1939, 29 Macchi MC 200s had been delivered, of which 25 were assigned to front-line units, while the others were assigned to flight training schools.

At the time of Italy's entry into the war on 10 June 1940, the number of MC 200s in the Regia Aeronautica was 156, with the 16th autonomous ground fighter group, the 181st squadron of the 6th fighter group of the 1st ground fighter wing in Sicily, the 152nd and 153rd groups of the 54th wing in Vergiate .

- At the same time, there were 118 FIAT G. 50 and 300 FIAT CR 42 available.

The transition to the new fighter aroused some resistance among the pilots, so much so that we can recall the case of the 4th Wing which, the first to receive the new fighters at the end of 1939, preferred to return to the trusty CR.42 biplanes when it was sent to fight in Libya in June 1940.

The reason for this downgrading was that the pilots of the 4th Wing were all veterans of the Spanish Civil War, or had years of experience in aerobatic displays all over the world, and were much more accustomed to their FIAT CR 32 and CR 42 biplanes: when they received the latest generation monoplane fighters, they did not have enough time to train adequately on them, and subsequently refused the opportunity to fly the Macchi MC 200.

- It should also be underlined that the pilots of the 4th Wing were the only ones who initially did not appreciate the Macchi.

On 23 October 1939, a few weeks after delivery, General Velardi , commander of another air unit, wrote to the General Staff of the Royal Italian Army declaring that his pilots were more than satisfied with the new aircraft and that within a few weeks of training they would be able to use the new Macchi for aerobatic displays.

- The first victim of the new Macchi MC 200 was a British four-engined flying boat Short S.25 Sunderland on a reconnaissance mission on 1 November 1940, near Augusta in Sicily.

With the arrival, towards the end of December, of the X Fliegerkorps in Sicily, the Macchis were assigned to escort the Ju 87s of I/ StG.1 and II/ StG.2 in their missions over Malta: at that time, in fact, the German Stukas did not yet have adequate protection, as the Messerschmitts had not yet arrived. Bf 109 of 7./JG 26.

During these missions, the Saettas proved to be effective and without particular defects in air combat against the Hawkers. Hurricane , also managing to outclass the old Gloster biplanes Gladiator without too much difficulty.

In Sicily, two Saettas from the 70th Squadron of the 23rd Autonomous Fighter Group, based at Boccadifalco airport , were used for night missions.

- Lieutenant Colonel Tito Falconi, commander of the group, and Captain Claudio Solaro , commander of the squadron, were the only ones to pilot the two Macchis at night.

According to the documents, between September and December 1941, these two fighters flew dozens of missions over Palermo, also participating in several clashes against British aircraft, but without managing to shoot down any. By the end of the year, the 23rd Group was sent back to Turin Mirafiori airport to be reorganized.

After the North African campaign, in July 1943, the Allied troops invaded Sicily : at that time, the Regia Aeronautica had 81 Macchi MC 200, 41 with the 2° Stormo, 3 in the 22° Gruppo, 13 in the 157° Gruppo, 4 in the 161° Gruppo and 20 aircraft in the 82° and 392° Squadrons.

- One of the last battles took place a few days before the armistice of Cassibile in September 1943.

On September 2, 1943, while on patrol near the naval base in the port of La Spezia, Lieutenant Petrosellini of the 92nd Squadron of the 8th Group intercepted a group of 24 American Boeing B-17 Flying Fortresses that were approaching to bomb the port facilities and industrial areas of the city: Petrosellini carried out two attacks alone against the giant American bombers, managing to shoot down one and damage a second.

He then made an emergency landing at Sarzana airport due to damage sustained from heavy defensive fire.

- As of September 8, 1943, 33 Macchi MC 200s were in the ranks of the Regia Aeronautica.

Until September 1943, the Saetta was the most used Italian fighter on all fronts.

The first examples of its successor, the Macchi MC 202, entered front-line service at the end of September 1941, while the first examples of the Macchi MC 205V appeared in February 1943.

From the entry into the war in June 1940 until the surrender on 8 September, the MC 200 was the most widely used Italian fighter.

Operational in Greece, North Africa, Yugoslavia, the Mediterranean and Russia, where it achieved an excellent ratio of 88 enemy aircraft shot down against 15 lost, the Saetta could compete with the best Allied fighters, often emerging victorious.

By the end of 1941 the Spitfire was the only enemy fighter capable of outclassing the MC 200, although the P-40, and advanced versions of the Hurricane , could cause serious problems.

After that date, American fighters with superior performance began to progressively arrive, such as the P-47, P-38, P-39 and, above all, the P-51 Mustang: in the same way, the Soviets also replaced their antiquated aircraft with considerably more modern machines, in particular the Yak 3 and Yak 9.

The British had gradually withdrawn the Glosters Gladiators and Hurricanes , replacing them, in 1941 in Malta, subsequently on all fronts, with Spitfires and Curtiss P-40s, therefore, from 1941/1942 onwards the Saetta became progressively obsolete: furthermore, its light armament did not allow it to act effectively as an interceptor.

- After the armistice of 1943, of the 33 Macchi MC 200s operational at the time, 10 remained in the territories occupied by the Germans: not much is known about these 10 units, but it can be assumed that almost all were confiscated by the Luftwaffe .

Several Macchi MC 200s remained in service with the Aeronautica Nazionale Repubblicana for training purposes: some of these vehicles had probably been recovered from depots or hangars and put back into service after a period of overhaul.

- As many as 23 Macchi MC 200s managed to reach southern Italy after the armistice of 8 September 1943: almost all of them belonged to the 8th Group, which had escorted the fleet of the Royal Navy from La Spezia to Malta.

Leverano Fighter School , where they were used for training until maintenance could no longer be carried out.

Unfortunately, not much is known about the Macchi MC 200s in service with the Italian Air Force after the war: some of these, probably the surviving aircraft of the 23 Saettas used by the Italian Co-Belligerent Air Force, were kept in service using spare parts found throughout the Italian peninsula, some with new parts produced after the war.

- They were used until 1947.

Having become obsolete by the end of the war, the Macchi MC 200s were employed by the 2nd Squadron of the Lecce Fighter School for the training of a new generation of Italian fighter pilots.

Former Squadron Leader D. H. Clarke wrote in 1955, in one of his books, that, at Sorman , in North Africa, he came into possession of a Macchi MC 200, serial number MM 5285: after three days of overhaul, the British officer boarded the Macchi and took it to their base at El Ass .

Clarke stated that the Macchi had excellent visibility, a spacious interior with an open cab (which he regarded very favorably), was rustic but simple, and had comfortable controls. The engine was quiet and easy to maintain and the vehicle was very maneuverable.

- During a simulated fight against a Hawker Hurricane II, a Curtiss P-40 and a Spitfire V, could outperform all three: the disadvantages Clarke highlighted were the poor armament, although he considered the ammunition reserve adequate, and the problem of capsizing.

The RAF captured more aircraft during the war: some aircraft were captured intact in Sicily and used to train British pilots, familiarizing them with enemy aircraft.

Being one of the longest-lived and most produced aircraft of the Regia Aeronautica during the Second World War, it is easy to understand that the Macchi MC 200 had many camouflage schemes during its operational life on the various fronts on which it operated.

The prototypes, at the time of their test flights and their presentation to the Army General Staff in Guidonia , had no camouflage or paint applied, with the natural aluminium exposed.

- On the rudder, there was the Italian Tricolour with the symbol of the Savoy family in the centre: this was the flag of the Kingdom of Italy until 1947.

On the side of the cockpit, there was the Fascio Littorio painted inside a round frame with a blue background.

On both sides of the wings there were also the "Fasci Littori Alari", circular rosettes 96 cm in diameter with a black outline and white background inside which were painted 3 stylised Fasci Littori: as the war progressed, the Fasci Littori Alari were slightly modified, those in the lower part were painted white, with a black background.

- The first examples produced by Macchi and then used in Italy and those used in the Soviet Union were painted dark green with dark brown spots with yellow outlines, but there were some variations: for example, the brown spots could be covered by small yellow spots or, as in the case of the 79th Squadron of the 6th Group of the 1st Wing, the dark green background was covered by yellow and brown spots.

Starting in June 1940, the aircraft of the Regia Aeronautica received a new characteristic: to avoid friendly fire incidents, the Italian Tricolour, which could be confused with the tricolour of French aircraft, was replaced by the Croce di

Savoia, symbol of the Italian royal family of Savoy, a white cross by ministerial order.

Furthermore, the Macchi, Breda and, later, SIA Ambrosini production plants painted the crosses differently.

- Macchi painted a cross with longer vertical arms.
- Breda painted a Greek cross, all arms of equal length.
- SIA Ambrosini painted the cross across the entire height of the rudder.

The Savoy Cross of different origins, the 1st from Macchi, the 2nd from Breda, the 3rd from SAI Ambrosini and, finally, the 4th is an example made by a department.

The white band on the fuselage was introduced in early 1941 for the same purpose.

Between the spring and summer of 1941, a regulation issued by the Ministry of War ordered that all fighters of the Regia Aeronautica were to be painted with a yellow nose to avoid friendly fire incidents, but the order lasted only a few months : in this case too, the dispatch was misunderstood and some units, especially in the Soviet Union, painted the fuselage line and wingtips yellow.

- The two aircraft of the 70th Squadron of the 23rd Autonomous Group were repainted by the unit completely in pitch black, which also covered all the markings.

In North Africa, there were many camouflage patterns, all on a khaki base with dark green spots.

After the fall of fascism in Italy, on 25 July 1943, pilots were ordered to obscure the Fascio Littorio, which was covered with the paint the units had available.

After the armistice of 8 September 1943, some Macchi MC 200s remained in the hands of Italian pilots fighting for the Italian Co-Belligerent Air Force, they were ordered to cover the tricolour emblem on the wings and fuselage and to obscure all previous insignia, such as the white band on the fuselage, the unit's emblem and the Savoy Cross.

- After the war, the few surviving examples were used in aluminium colour with tricolour cockades on the fuselage and wings.

The examples captured by the British and Americans had the Allied emblem to cover the Italian ones. For example, the American example retained the squadron identification numbers, but all other symbols were obscured or covered with American symbols.

United insignia. States Army Air Forces .

After the armistice of 8 September 1943, the German Army managed to recover a small number of Macchi MC 200s from Italian airfields and put them into service with the Luftwaffe , mostly as training aircraft.

As far as is known, these never took part in actions against Allied targets.

Yugoslavia

At the outbreak of hostilities against Yugoslavia, the only air units assigned to the sector were the 4th Wing, equipped with 96 Macchi MC 200s, the 7th Group at Treviso and the 16th Group at Ravenna, which had 22 each, the 9th Group at Gorizia and the 10th Group at Altura di Pola , which had 23 each, and, finally, 6 which were in service with the 256th Squadron at Bari.

At dawn on 6 April 1941, before the declaration of war, four MC 200s of the 73rd Squadron took off without a specific mission, flew over the port of Pola and then reached the island of Cres , attacking a tanker and setting it on fire.

- There were no notable actions for the remainder of the short Yugoslav campaign.

The Macchis of the 4th Stormo flew against Yugoslavia for the last time on 14 April, when 20 Saettas of the 10th Gruppo patrolled the airspace 100 km south of Karlovac , but without encountering enemy aircraft.

In March 1941, to counter the new Hawkers British Hurricanes , the Regia Aeronautica was forced to withdraw the FIAT CR 42s of the 150° Gruppo from Albania, replacing them with 36 Macchi MC 200s of the 22° Gruppo stationed at Tirana airport and of the 371° Squadron, which moved from Rome-Ciampino airport to Valona .

Despite its lower top speed than the Hurricanes , in the hands of experienced and well-trained Italian pilots in aerobatics, the Macchi MC 200 proved a difficult opponent for British pilots.

- Ground operations on the Yugoslav front ended on 17 April.

According to the official report of the 4th Wing, in eleven days there were no losses, 4 enemy aircraft were shot down and 45 Yugoslavian aircraft were destroyed on the ground, damaging ten others.

Further victories were achieved by destroying an oil tanker, a tanker and an unknown number of mechanized vehicles, as well as destroying airport facilities.

Another 5 Yugoslavian aircraft, Dornier Do 17Ks, were destroyed on the ground at a Greek airfield where they had taken refuge during an Italian attack.

After the attack on Yugoslavia, on 12 June 1941 the 10th Group was transferred to Sicily, to Catania, for a series of operations against Malta: during this period, all the Fiat A.74 engines, produced under licence by Reggiane, after an inspection by a captain of the Air Force Engineering Corps and an engineer of the company, were replaced due to faults that brought the oil temperatures to dangerous levels.

North Africa

For the Macchi MC 200, the desert was the most important theatre of operations.

At the end of operations in Yugoslavia, the 153° Gruppo returned to Italy. It was based at Grottaglie airfield in southern Italy, with the task of defending the port of Taranto from RAF attacks.

- One of its squadrons, however, was ordered to North Africa to support Rommel's offensive in Cyrenaica.

The first eleven MC200s of the 374th Squadron, under the command of Captain Andrea Favini , who would later become squadron leader, arrived on 19 April 1941 at Castel Benito airport, 35 km south of Tripoli: at the end of June only nine remained.

During its period of activity, the squadron never reached more than 7 operational Macchis at the same time.

An interesting fact is that Captain Andrea Favini was still using a pre-production Macchi MC 200 with a FIAT-Hamilton 34D-1 nose cone and propellers.

pre-production aircraft , and the very first production run, would have had to be modified by that point.

On 2 July 1941, the Macchi MC 200 of the 372nd Squadron of the famous 153rd "Asso di Bastoni" Group arrived in North Africa: the 153rd Group's July-December total was 359 actions for a total of 4,686 hours and 54 opponents destroyed on the ground and in flight.

- Later, the 373rd Squadron from Greece also arrived, together with the 157th Group.

The 76th Squadron of the 7th Autonomous Land Fighter Group, commanded by Major Marcello Fossetta, also arrived with 22 Macchi MC 200s: however, they lost almost all of their fighters during a British air attack on the Benina base , 19 km east of Benghazi, where the unit was based.

On 8 December 1941, a Macchi MC200 of the 153° Gruppo clashed with the Hawkers Hurricane of the British 974 Squadron. During one engagement, a Macchi engaged a Hurricane . After a series of very tight turns, the Macchi hit the cockpit of the Hawker , which then rolled over and nose-dived, killing New Zealand RAF Flight Lieutenant Owen Vincent Tracey , who had 6 credited victories to his name.

- In December 1941, the Macchi MC 200 began to be accompanied by the Macchi MC 202 of the 8th and 150th Groups stationed at El-Nofilia airport .

In the early months of 1942, the 8th, 13th and 150th Groups were mainly employed in escort missions for FIAT CR 42s in ground attack configuration.

On 20 July 1942, the 18th Group of the 3rd Wing arrived in Tripoli with the 83rd, 85th and 95th squadrons: forty aircraft in total, of which 21 in the MC 200CB configuration, equipped with two wing bomb racks weighing 3 kg, for loads of up to 160 kg, although four 15 kg ones were often attached.

These new arrivals, which were positioned at the Abu-Aggag air base , 370 km from Cairo, meant that the Macchi 200 was still the most numerous Italian fighter in North Africa, with 76 units, of which approximately three-quarters were operational, 37 of which in the 2nd Wing.

The Macchi MC 200CB of the 18th Group carried out dozens of ground attack missions.

- One of the most famous was stopping the British attempt to recapture Tobruk by sea in July 1942, sinking the destroyer Zulu and severely damaging two troop transports.

On 18 April 1942, between 17.25 and 18.30, five Macchi MC 200CBs attacked a column of tanks of the 1st Armoured Division of the British 8th Army at Sidi Bou Ali, in the governorate of Susa , Tunisia. 22 MC 202s of the 54° Stormo escorting the "Saetta" clashed with a formation of P-40s and Spitfires that had arrived to support the armoured units: Captain Sergio Maurer , Lieutenant Giuseppe Robetto and Sergeant Mauri each shot down a Spitfire , while Sergeant Rodoz shot down a P-40.

- Despite the Regia Aeronautica's gradual transition to the Macchi MC 202, the Saetta remained the most widely used fighter aircraft, and was also widely used as a secondary fighter by pilots when their MC 202s were under repair.

The 364th Squadron of the 150th Fighter Group, 52nd Wing, equipped with the Macchi MC 200 'Saetta', operating from the El Agheila , Bengasi and Martuba , participated intensively in interception operations, surveillance flights, strafing of ground targets and escorting bombers.
The Macchi MC 200s were also able to successfully engage Allied four-engined aircraft, despite their armament.
On August 14, Lieutenant Vallauri of the 2nd Wing intercepted four Consolidated B-24 Liberators during a reconnaissance mission in the skies above Tobruk : instead of waiting for support from other fighters, he attacked them alone, managing to shoot down one.
A few days later, on 23 August 1942, three MC 200s intercepted and attacked a group of B-24 Liberators en route to Tobruk . Sergeant Zanarini and Second Lieutenant Zuccarini shot down one Liberator while the third pilot damaged another.

- The unit's tally, that August, was 198 aircraft employed in 394 hours on Tobruk , with 1,482 hours of escorts to 77 convoys.

But the Allied superiority was becoming increasingly overwhelming.

In October, the Macchi 200s lost by the 2nd Stormo were ten, and at the beginning of November 1942, the Saettas on the front line, between the 2nd and 3rd Stormo, were only 15: this was a very limited number considering that in July, there were 76, which meant an average loss rate of around 12 aircraft per month.

Although outclassed in speed and armament by the latest versions of the Hawker Hurricanes , Curtiss P-40s and, above all, Supermarine Spitfires , the Macchis still managed to obtain some victories: in November, Lieutenant Savoia and Sergeant Major Baldi shot down two Bristol Beaufighters , while Sergeant Turchetti managed to shoot down two aircraft.

- But on December 1st the 2nd Wing had only 42 Saettas in its ranks, of which 19 were efficient.

On March 29, 1943, in the Gabès sector, North Africa, fifteen MC 200s intercepted P-40s and Spitfires, claiming 4 victories at the cost of a forced landing.

After the battle of El Alamein, the Macchis were used to cover the retreat of the Italo-German troops : however, the lack of spare parts, fuel and the overwhelming technological and numerical superiority of the Allies meant that many aircraft were lost.

In October 1942, the 18° Gruppo received the Macchi MC 202s of the 4° Stormo, which, after months of action, had been repatriated for reorganization.

- On 11 January 1943, units of the 3rd Wing were employed in the attack against some British air bases in the Wadi Tamet area .

The Macchi MC 202s escorted the Macchi MC 200CB fighter-bombers in bombing operations: Luigi Gorrini managed to shoot down the Spitfire Mark V of Flying Officer Neville Duke of the 92nd Squadron, as reported by the British pilot himself in one of his books.

By January 1943, all non-operational units were repatriated, with very few Macchi MC 200s remaining in North Africa as part of the 384th Squadron at Tunis and the 13th and 18th Groups at El Hamam .

The last group to be equipped with MC 200s was the 18th Group of Major Mario Becich , which fought with the Saetta until the end of the campaign.

The last major air battle of the Macchi MC 200s in North Africa was on 29 March 1943: then, in the Gabès sector, 15 MC 200s from various units intercepted an unknown number of P-40s and Spitfires , shooting down 4 enemy aircraft at the cost of one damaged aircraft forced to land on the way back.

Malta

Malta, a British stronghold in the Mediterranean, was the scene of dozens of air battles in which the Macchi MC 200s took part.

- Just over the island of Malta, on 23 June 1940, the first loss of an MC 200 was recorded, a victim of the Royal Air Force .

Nine Macchi MC 200s of the 79th Squadron, eight of the 88th Squadron and one of the 81st Squadron, all belonging to the 6th Group, escorted ten Savoia Marchetti SM.79s of the 11th Bomber Wing towards the island.

Immediately, the British launched two Glosters Gladiator to intercept them.

Sergeant Major Molinelli, of 71 Squadron, attacked one of two British aircraft which, in turn, were attacking a bomber off Sliema .

- The Macchi 200 was hit and fell into the sea: it is unclear whether Major Molinelli survived.

Franco Lucchini, an Italian ace of the 90th Squadron of the 10th Fighter Group of the 4th Wing with 26 victories, took off on 27 June 1941 from Trapani airport in Sicily: he was engaged in an attack mission during which he shot down a Hawker Hurricane : later, he shared many other victories with his companions of the 4th Wing.

Another recorded loss occurred on the morning of 25 July 1941, when approximately 40 Macchi MC 200s of the 54° Stormo were tasked with escorting a CANT Z.1007bis of the 30° Stormo for a photographic reconnaissance over La Valletta: the mission was aimed at photographing a British naval convoy that had been attacked the day before by torpedo bombers.

- Over the island, about 30 Hurricanes slammed into the formation, bringing down CANT Z. 1007 bis in flames.

Second Lieutenant Liberti's Saetta was shot down, with the loss of the pilot, as well as that of Lieutenant De Giorgi, whose fate is unknown.

Italian fighter pilots claimed four Hurricanes shot down , two by Sergeant Major Magnaghi , one by Captain Gostini and one by Sergeant Omiccioli of the 98th Squadron.

On 27 October 1940, Carlo Poggio Suasa of the 81st Squadron, 6th Group, assigned to the 1st Land Fighter Wing based at Catania-Fontanarossa airport , shot down a Hawker Hurricane over Malta.

- On 11 July 1941, during an attack on the Maltese air base of Micabba , three Italian aces, belonging to the 10° Gruppo of the 4° Stormo, were engaged by seven or eight enemy Hurricanes .

They were Leonardo Ferrulli , with 21 victories, Carlo Romagnoli, 11 victories and 6 probables, and Franco Lucchini, 22 victories: after an exhausting aerial combat, the three MC 200s managed to disengage and were chased for 40 km before the British gave up the pursuit and, with their aircraft damaged but still able to fly, managed to return to Sicily safe and sound.

On 27 June 1941, the same units of the 10th Group, 4th Wing, commanded by the ace Carlo Romagnoli, took off from Catania-Fontanarossa airport in Sicily to escort a Savoia-Marchetti SM 79 on a reconnaissance mission: once they reached Malta, they were immediately intercepted by a group of Hawker Hurricane Mark I of No. 46 Squadron RAF which forced them to abandon the mission and return to Sicily.

- On 4 September, Romagnoli led a reconnaissance mission over Malta with a formation of 17 MC 200s.

Their goal was to confirm the sinking of a merchant ship that had been hit that night by a Junkers Ju 87B of the 101st Autonomous Dive Bombardment Group piloted by Sergeant Major Valentino Zagnoli , near Kalafrana .

- Having arrived in Valletta, the Macchi carried out a reconnaissance of the port at 6,000 metres and, having found nothing, returned to Sicily.

At this point, 21 Hawker fighters Hurricane Mark IIs of No. 126 and No. 185 Squadrons were waiting for them, thanks to Maltese radar, at about 7,500 metres.

After the furious battle that followed, Second Lieutenant Andrea Della Pasqua of the 91st Squadron was reported missing after being seen parachuting: he was never found.

The 76th Squadron of the 7th Group of the 5th Land Fighter Wing took part in the Battle of Pantelleria between 12 and 15 June 1942.

There, Axis forces, with 92 Regia Aeronautica and 48 Luftwaffe aircraft , destroyed two and damaged four merchant ships at a cost of 29 aircraft lost and 12 pilots killed.

- Since the three-engined reconnaissance aircraft flying over Malta were easy targets, some mechanics modified about ten Macchi MC 200s with an Avia RB 20/75/30 camera positioned behind the pilot's seat.

This strategy reduced the fighter's top speed, but made the reconnaissance aircraft unrecognizable to the enemy, as well as being much more agile and faster than the trimotor aircraft they replaced.

Some examples assigned to the 1st Fighter Wing, belonging to the first production series, were withdrawn from the front line due to problems caused by defective wing profiles.

Once this shortcoming was corrected, the Macchi 200 proved to be a reliable machine.

Very easy to handle, it still had enough speed to compete with the Hawker Hurricane , which was superior in maneuver combat, but surpassed in firepower.

The maneuverability and the robustness of the structure and the radial engine were the only resources of the "Saetta" which, only thanks to the experience of the pilots, managed to obtain some aerial victories.

- One of the last occurred a few days before the Armistice.

On September 3, 1943, (or more likely September 2, 1943) while on patrol at the naval base in the port of La Spezia, Lieutenant Petrosellini of the 92nd Squadron of the 8th Group was put on alert by the fighter guide.

A squadron of 24 American Boeing B-17 Flying Fortresses was approaching: Petrosellini carried out two attacks alone, encountering the classic violent barrage of B-17s, managing to shoot down one and then making an emergency landing on his airfield at Sarzana.

Russia

A contingent of Macchi MC 200s was sent to the front in the Soviet Union, despite having an open cockpit.

The Aviation Command of the Italian Expeditionary Force in Russia was officially established on 29 July 1941 at Tudora airport .

Borzoni 's Group landed at this airport on 12 August with Captain Vittorio Minguzzi 's 359th Squadron , which had 11 other pilots, including Captain Carlo Miani and Lieutenant Giovanni Bonet .

Ferla 's 362nd Squadron also arrived with 11 other pilots.

It was followed by the 369th Squadron, commanded by Captain Giorgio Jannicelli , with 13 pilots, and, finally, the 371st Squadron of Captain Enrico Meille , with 11 pilots, all belonging to the 22nd Autonomous Land Fighter Group.

On 16 August the 61st Air Observation Group also arrived, with 32 Caproni Ca.311s and a Savoia-Marchetti SM82 as support.

- The 22nd Group therefore had a total of 51 MC 200s.

The Italians carried out their first missions from Krivoi Rog on 27 August 1941, scoring eight aerial victories against Soviet fighters and bombers, two Poliakov I-16s and six Tupolev SB-2s.

Due to the lightning advance of Axis troops into the Soviet Union, at the end of August, the unit had to move to Kryvyi Rih airfield. Rih and Zaporizhia by the end of September. On 9 November, the 371st Squadron moved to the Donetsk sector , breaking away from the rest of the group.

Between August and early December, 22nd Group shot down another 8 Soviet fighters and bombers, apparently without suffering any losses, while another 4 Soviets were shot down in December.

A Macchi MC 200 in Russia in 1942 with two 100 kg bombs in underwing mounts.

During the Soviet Christmas ground offensive against Italian troops at Novo Orlovka , Italian pilots attacked Soviet troops in the Burlova sector : during these actions, they also shot down five Soviet fighters without suffering any losses.

- During one of these missions, on 28 December, Macchis of the 359th Squadron shot down nine Soviet aircraft in the Timofeyevka and Polskaya areas , including six Polikarpov I-16 fighters and three bombers, without suffering any losses.

On December 29, 1941 , the 369th Squadron lost its commander, Captain Giorgio Jannicelli : during a solo reconnaissance mission, he was intercepted by more than ten I-

16 and MiG-3 fighters and, after a grueling air battle, was shot down: for his courage, he was posthumously awarded the Gold Medal.

The Italian Macchi in the Soviet Union were unable to carry out any missions throughout January and the first days of February 1942 due to bad weather.

What this first Russian winter was like for the units of our air force and in particular for the MC 200 units, is well illustrated by a page from the diary of the 371st squadron , compiled on 6 December 1941 by Captain Enrico Meille at Stalino airport :

- The cover sheets are insufficient.
- The stoves themselves and the hot air conveyors are insufficient.
- Freezing of petrol emission lines due to low engine speed operation.
- Need to preheat starter motors and, for much longer, engine oil.
- Freezing in the hydraulic control pump.
- Freezing of oil in the hydraulic circuit of the landing gear resulting in the inability to retract once in flight.
- Specialists working in temperatures below 30°, subject to frostbite on limbs and faces.
- Pilots who find even lower temperatures in open cockpits at high altitude and for which even the heated suits prove insufficient, with consequent frostbite.
- Airplane windshields, reflective sights for shooting, even the pilots' glasses, permanently fogged up with a very modest reduction in visibility.

On February 4 and 5, the Regia Aeronautica launched an operation to destroy Soviet air bases. The first was at Kranyi Liman , where the MC 200 destroyed 21 Soviet aircraft on the ground and another 5 fighters were shot down during dogfights over the airfield.

- Luskotova and Leninsklij airfields were also attacked. To kiss .

By the end of March 1942, 22 Group had achieved another 21 aerial victories against the Soviet Air Force.

On 4 May 1942, the 22nd Group, which still had some operational aircraft, was replaced by the 21st Group, composed of the 356th, 382nd, 361st and 386th Squadrons.

The 21st, commanded by Major Ettore Foschini , brought with it 12 new Macchi MC 202 fighters and 18 new Macchi MC 200s, probably the fighter-bomber version.

During the Second Battle of Kharkov , fought between 12 and 30 May 1942, Italian pilots flew escort missions for German scouts and bombers.

They earned the admiration of the commander of the German 17th Army, especially for their bold and effective attacks in the Slavyansk area against Soviet fighters trying to shoot down German bombers.

- In the summer of 1942, following the German advance, the 21st Group moved first to Makeyevka airfield and later to Tazinskaya , Voroshilovgrad and Oblivskaya airfields , shooting down 5 enemy aircraft in May, 5 in June and 11 in July.

Increasingly, Italian pilots were asked to escort German aircraft, but the Macchi aircraft wore out very quickly due to lack of spare parts, and on 25 and 26 July, five MC200s were shot down during air combat with the Soviets.

In the summer, 17 Macchi 202s arrived from Italy to reinforce the Saette formation, now worn out by incessant use.

At the beginning of December, the Macchi MC 200s still in service were 32 supported by 11 Macchi MC 202s, but the losses suffered became increasingly consistent, due to the technological progress of the Soviet aircraft.

- On 6 August 1942, some MC 200CBs flew a bombing mission east of the Don, hitting Soviet artillery and infantry with their 50 kg bombs.

In December, only 32 Macchi MC 200s were available and 11 Macchi MC 202s.

The Soviet Air Force, which was beginning to be better trained for combat, as well as the increasing prevalence of anti-aircraft fire caused further losses: in fact, over half of the missions the Macchis were required to carry out were ground attacks against Soviet tanks and infantry.

The last Italian action employing large numbers of aircraft was on 17 January 1943, when 25 Macchi MC 200s and MC 202s strafed troops on the ground in the Millerovo sector .

On 18 January 1943, Commander Ettore Foschini received orders to retreat, first to Stalino airfield in Donetsk , and from there to Zaporizhia .

- On 20 February 1943, the Group was at Odessa air base, waiting to return to Italy, and on 15 April the Group left Odessa and, after four stopovers, arrived at Peretola airport in Florence at the end of the month.

Thirty Macchi MC 200s and nine MC 202s returned to Italy, while 15 unserviceable aircraft were abandoned during the retreat.

A total of 66 Italian aircraft had been lost on the Eastern Front due to various causes, compared , according to official data, with 88 enemy aircraft shot down, during 17 months of action in that theatre of war.

Compendium of operations:

- 2,557 offensive penetration flights
- 511 in tactical support with bomb dropping

- 1,310 machine gun fire
- 1,938 stocks
- 88 opponents destroyed with the loss of 15 Macchi MC 200s.
- The leading unit was the 362nd Squadron led by Captain Germano La Ferlache , which destroyed 13 Soviet aircraft on the ground and shot down 30 in flight.

Greece

For the air combat during the Greek campaign, which began on 28 October 1940, the 54th Wing was employed, composed as follows:

- The 372nd Squadron, based at Brindisi-Casale airport, had 12 Macchi MC 200s.
- The 373rd Squadron, with 11 MC 200s, was at Bari-Palese airport.
- The 374th Squadron, with 12 MC 200s, at Taranto-Grottaglie airport .
- The 370th, with 8 MC 200, at Foggia airport.

These squadrons mainly performed escort missions for the Italian FIAT BR 20 and Savoia-Marchetti SM 79 bombers used against Greek strategic targets.

Sergeant Luigi Gorrini of the 85th Squadron of the 18th Fighter Group of the 3rd Land Fighter Wing, an Italian ace with 19 confirmed victories and 9 presumed victories, attended training courses to learn how to fly the Macchi MC 200 and FIAT G. 50 held at the Caselle Torinese and Turin Mirafiori airfields between 29 August and 10 December 1940.

After that, he and his squadron were transferred to Araxos airfield in Greece, where he performed escort flights for naval and air convoys from Italy to Greece and vice versa.

On 17 December 1940, while patrolling the island of Cephalonia, Gorrini sighted two Bristol Blenheims , hitting one, which he considered probably shot down, and damaging the second.

In March 1941, the 22nd Independent Ground Fighter Group was sent to Greece.

His 371 Squadron went to Valona , while the rest of the group, with 36 Macchi MC 200s and an unknown number of FIAT CR.42s, moved to Tirana airport, both cities in occupied Albania.

During their first battles, they clashed with the Hawkers Hurricanes and the Glosters RAF Gladiator .

Thanks to reinforcements arriving in Albania in April, the 18th Group was sent back to Italy to train on the Macchi MC 200CB.

- Training lasted until mid-July, when the Greek campaign was over.

The Group was subsequently transferred to North Africa.

During the Greek campaign, which lasted until April 1941, Royal Air Force fighters Italian Air Force claimed to have shot down 77 Hellenic Air Force aircraft , plus another 24 presumed, of which 52 were shot down and 25 destroyed on the ground, for a loss of 64 Italian aircraft.

During the clashes with the RAF, the British claimed to have destroyed 93 Italian aircraft, and another 26 probables, for only 10 aircraft lost.

However, by the end of the campaign, British losses amounted to 150 pilots, killed or taken prisoner, and 209 aircraft lost, 72 shot down by Italian fighters, 55 destroyed on the ground and 82 destroyed or abandoned during the evacuation.

16th group

The 16th Group was a flight group of the Aeronautical Service of the Royal Army, active in the First and Second World Wars.

It was founded in Sovizzo on 16 December 1917 and was formed from the 31st Squadron, the 71st Fighter Squadron and the 121st Squadron, and was part of the Air Force Command of the 1st Army under the interim command of Captain Amerigo Notari who commanded the [71st].

At the end of December it received the 1st SVA Section and on 4 January 1918 the interim position passed to Capt. Giulio Palma di Cesnola .

Pomilio Squadron arrives and at the beginning of April the interim position passes to Captain Observer Franco Scarioni of the 31st.

Castelgomberto airfield with the squadrons.

On May 29 the command returned to Palma di Cesnola and in July the 135th was [disbanded] .

On August 14, command passes to Captain Ercole Messi, on September 4 the 134th B Squadron arrives and on September 23 the 71st [cedes] .

In December he went to Bolzano di San Giovanni al Natisone and on 28 February 1919 he was with the 31st and the 11th.

It was dissolved on 1 August 1919.

In April 1937 the 16th "Cucaracha" Group of the Legionary Aviation was formed which included:

- The 24th Squadron, formerly 1st Escuadrilla de Caza del Tercio or Cucaracha Squadron.
- The 25th Squadron, previously 2nd.
- The 26th Squadron, previously 3rd, on Fiat CR.32s at Cáceres (Spain).

On August 3, 1937, the XVI Group "La Cucaracha" was still operating in the Spanish Civil War.

On 17 January 1938, promoted to the rank of Major Armando François, he replaced Major Casero in command of the 16th Fighter Group, stationed at the Saragossa-Sanjurjo airport .

On March 6 he was replaced by Major Ciro Aiello , but, just as he was preparing to return to Italy, Major Aiello was shot down on March 14, and he had to resume command of the group, which he held until August 10, when he was replaced by Lieutenant Colonel Arrigo Tessari .

On the afternoon of 23 May, the 28 Fiat CR.32s of the 16° Gruppo escorted 20 S.79 Sparviero bombers and five BR.20 Cocogna to the Balaguer beachhead in Catalonia, in support of the Spanish Nationalist army.

- During the fighting that day he shot down a Polikarpov I-16 fighter.

On the morning of August 5th he led into action the three squadrons of the 16th Group, with a total of 30 Fiqat CR .32, intercepting six Tupolev SBs of the 3rd " Katiuska " Squadron , escorted by 21 I-16 fighters, which were approaching the Nationalist positions from the north-east, crossing the river line over Cherta .

During the following combat he claimed the shared destruction of an SB, whose crew bailed out and landed in the Republican zone.

- On 10 August 1938, Tessari became commander of the 16th Fighter Group "La Cucaracha", of the 3rd Fighter Wing of the Aviazione Legionaria based in Caspe .

As his first follower he had Sergeant Major Giuseppe Biron : in December 1938 his Group was assigned to support the Nationalist advance on Barcelona.

With the end of the civil war he returned to Italy.

Until 1938, the 16th Group flew with the 168th and 169th Squadrons with Caproni AP1s in the 50th Assault Wing.

On 10 June 1940 the unit was in Sorman under the command of Major Spartaco Sella with the Breda Ba.65s of the 167th on six BA 65s and 168th Squadron on five BA 65s in the 50th Assault Wing of the Libyan Air Force - West.

In relation to the operations linked to the Invasion of Yugoslavia in April 1941, it went on alert as a fighter unit from Ravenna Airport with 22 Macchi MC 200s of the 2nd Air Squadron.

In February 1943 he was at the Medenine airport in Tunisia on the Macchi MC202, later moving to the 54th Wing.

21st Group

The 21st Autonomous Ground Fighter Group, or simply 21st Fighter Group, was a group of the Regia Aeronautica that fought on the Russian and Italian fronts during the Second World War.

Angry Vespa symbol of the 21st Group

On 4 May 1942 the 21st Group, composed of the 356th, 382nd, 361st and 386th Squadrons, replaced the 22nd Group, while the 71st Aerial Observation Group on Caproni Ca.311s, composed of the 38th and 116th Squadrons, replaced the 61st Group.
The groups were included in the newly formed 8th Italian Army in Russia (ARM.IR) consisting of approximately 227,000 men under the command of General Italo Gariboldi .
The 21st Group, commanded by Major Ettore Foschini , was equipped with 18 new Macchi MC 200s.
During the Second Battle for Kharkov (12-30 May), the Italians carried out numerous support flights for German bombers.

In May, the pilots of the 21st Group received praise from the commander of the German 17th Army, especially for their bold and effective attacks in the Slavyansk area .

During the German advance in the summer of 1942, the 21st Group was transferred to Makeyevka and later to Voroshilovgrad and Oblivskaya .

Increasingly, the Macchis were tasked with escorting German aircraft and on 25 and 26 July 1942, five MC200s were lost in aerial combat.

From late spring 1943 the Group was engaged in Italy and was involved in air operations against the Landing in Sicily.

- Following the events of 8 September 1943 the group was dissolved.

The 22nd Independent Ground Fighter Group, or simply 22nd Fighter Group, was a group of the Regia Aeronautica that fought on the Russian front during the Second World War.

- The 22nd Group was sent to the front in the summer of 1941 with four squadrons made up of veteran pilots, the 359th, 362nd, 369th and 371st.

The Group remained at the front until May 1942, when it was replaced by the 21st Independent Land Fighter Group. Starting in 1953, the 22nd Group was annexed to the 51st Wing of the refounded Italian Republic Air Force.

The Aviation Command of the Italian Expeditionary Force in Russia was officially established on 29 July 1941 at Tudora airport : the Group landed at this airport on 12 August.

The aircraft were 51 Macchi MC200s which adopted a Mediterranean camouflage: light ochre background, with a dense network of irregular dull green spots, while the engine cowling, the band on the fuselage just behind the cockpit and the lower edge of the wingtip were yellow.

On the leading edge of the wings appeared two large white triangles, with the tips pointing towards the inside of the wing.

- The identification and squadron numbers were painted black.

The Macchis were accompanied by two Savoia-Marchetti SM.81s and three Caproni Ca.133s for logistical support.

On August 16, the 61st Air Observation Group also arrived with 32 Caproni Ca.311s (34th, 119th, and 128th squadrons) and a Savoia-Marchetti SM82 for support.

On 27 August the Group carried out its baptism of fire by shooting down eight Soviet aircraft, two Polikarpov I-16s and six Tupolev SB-2s, without suffering any losses.

In the following days the Soviets no longer flew their aircraft, which were too old compared to the Macchis.

The Italians therefore thought they had frightened the enemy, hence the adoption of the scarecrow smoking enemy planes, represented by eight red stars.

The Group's emblem was, in fact, a scarecrow on a white triangle.

The 22nd Group returned to Italy on 4 May 1942, leaving the aircraft to the incoming 21st Group.

At the end of June it will be deployed again in Sardinia with the new Reggiane Re.2001 and then in Sicily, under the command of Major Vittorio Minguzzi .

- Then the department will move on to defend Naples.

Starting from the spring of 1943, one of the group's squadrons, the 362nd, will be in charge of some brand new pre- series Reggiane Re.2005s, which it will use in interception missions together with the Macchi MC.202s, the Reggiane Re. 2001s and the Dewoitine D.520s already in charge.
  - The first pilot to take the new fighter into combat will be Group Commander Major Minguzzi .

After the war, the 22nd Group, renamed Interceptor Group, was integrated into the 51st Wing and operated with the F-104S interceptor fighters and, from 1989, the F-104ASA.
In 1995 he received the silver and bronze medals for military valor for his activities during the Second World War.
On 25 February 1999, as part of the measures aimed at reorganising the Air Force, the group was placed in a "framework position", while the last aircraft and part of the personnel were inherited by the XX Group of the 4th Wing.

4th Wing

The 4th Fighter Wing was born on 1 June 1931 at Udine-Campoformido Airport on Fiat CR.20 aircraft , incorporating into it some squadrons that had previously belonged to the 1st Wing, including the 91st, also known as the squadron of aces, as its pilots distinguished themselves during the First World War by collecting a high number of victories.
Among them, those with more than 10 victories were: Ferruccio Ranza , Luigi Olivari, Fulco Ruffo di Calabria, Pier Ruggero Piccio and the very famous Francesco Baracca.

The 4th Wing took its symbol, the prancing horse derived from the "historical patch" of its old "Piemonte Reale Cavalleria" Regiment, from the ace par excellence of the Royal Army Air Service, which would distinguish it to the present day.
At the end of May, the 84th and 91st Squadrons, incorporated into the 7th Independent Ground Fighter Group of Ciampino

South Airport, moved to Campoformido , home at that time of the 1st Fighter Wing: from this Wing were taken the 9th Fighter Group with the 73rd Squadron, the 96th and 97th and the 10th Group with the 90th Squadron, the 84th and 91st.

On September 9, the X Group which was at Aviano Airport, moved to Gorizia - Merna Airport , followed, on the 28th of the same month, by the IX and the Wing Command, and was equipped, among the first wings, with the CR Asso, a version with a more powerful engine of the Fiat CR.20 .

In January 1936, personnel from the 97th Squadron helped form the 150th Squadron of the 6th Wing at Campoformido ; in March, personnel and material from the 90th Squadron was moved to Turin-Mirafiori Airport to create the 366th Squadron of the 53rd Wing and in July the remaining strength of the 90th created the 367th Squadron of the 52nd Wing at Ghedi Airport . Among its pilots was also Aldo Remondino .

Between October 1931 and October 1932 it was commanded by Felice Porro and from May 1933 to March 1934 by Colonel Amedeo Duca D'Aosta. In 1935 it was equipped with Fiat CR.32s .

The following year, the Wing was employed in Italian East Africa and, subsequently, had its baptism of fire during the Spanish Civil War.

In 1939 it took part in the Italian invasion of Albania with 5 Caproni Ca.133 and from September it received the Fiat CR.42

.

At the outbreak of the Second World War, the 4th Wing of Colonel Cesare Caccianotti was at Gorizia Airport with the 9th Fighter Group of Major Ernesto Botto with the 73rd Squadron, with five CR 42s, the 96th with five CR 42s and the 97th Squadron with four CR 42s in the 2nd Land Fighter Division "Borea" of General BA Silvio Scaroni di Caselle of the 1st Air Squadron.

It was initially used on the Western Front, then in Sicily and, finally, in Cyrenaica (eastern Libya), where it could count on the new CR.42s .

On 10 June 1940 the 10th Group was at Tobruk T.2 Airport with the 84th Squadron, the 90th Squadron and the 91st Squadron with nine Fiat CR 42s, each under the command of Lt. Col. Armando Pieragino in the Libyan Air Force - East.

- On 13 July the Wing is, with both groups, at Berca Airport .

In the following December the wing returned to Italy with the 9th Group followed in January 1941 by the 10th Group. In 1941 on MC 200s the wing was redeployed to Sicily, from where it carried out raids on Malta and escort operations for transports.

On 1 January 1942 Armando François assumed command of the 4th Land Fighter Wing, which had just been re-equipped with Macchi MC 202 Folgore fighters.

- In April 1942, after suffering numerous losses, it was reconstituted in Sicily and Cyrenaica on the Macchi MC 202s.

Between 20 and 22 May, the Macchi of the "Cavallino Rampante" moved to North Africa; on 25 May, the 9th and 10th Group deployed at Martuba 4 Airport, one of the fields around Derna (Libya).

Its MC202s belonging to the 9th and 10th Groups took part in the Axis offensive of 26 May 1942 when, before dawn, nine Fiat CR.42s carried out an attack against the military airport of Gambut which was immediately hit by 59 MC 202s: 24 enemy fighters were hit during take-off.

From June it moves to Fuka (Sidi Militar Airport) Haneish) where on 20 October, the Royal Air Force carried out major attacks against the Wing.

The night of 25 August 1942 was perhaps the most successful night for Italian night fighters; Lieutenant Colonel François, commander of the 4th Wing, took off on a Fiat CR.42 , probably borrowed from the 238th Squadron, to counter the RAF night bombings on Fuka (Sidi Militar Airport). Haneish), in North Africa , intercepting and shooting down an unidentified twin-engine bomber which fell into the sea 4 km from the coast.

After landing, Lieutenant Giulio Reiner boarded the same aircraft and, guided by radio guidance, intercepted a Wellington (DV514/U) of No.70 Squadron RAF at 2,500 metres, again above Fuka .

Reiner hit the bomb bay of the bomber which crashed 10 km southeast of Fuka , exploding.

The Italian fighters engage in combat on October 20, and further combat on October 21, against enemy formations three or four times larger.

From 22 to 31 October, further clashes took place; the Italian fighter groups inflicted many losses on the enemy, but were unable to stop him and were therefore forced to leave the airport and retreat on 11 November to return to Martuba , when he had about ten operational aircraft left which he gave to the 3rd Wing to receive 28 MC 202s, which had arrived from Italy.

- On November 20, the wing was at Ara Fileni of Ras Lanuf . On December 6, the 9th group moved to the defense of the port of Tripoli, organized also using radio location systems.

At the beginning of 1943 the Wing received the MC 205 and in the summer of the same year it was employed in the defense of the mother country from the Anglo-American advance during the landing in Sicily. In the following October François left the command to Major Roberto Fassi . Alessandro Mettimanno , future Chief of Staff of the Air Force, between 1 September 1943 and April 1946 commanded the 84th Squadron of the Land Fighter Wing; for his war activity, Mettimanno was decorated with two silver medals and one bronze medal for military valor; he also obtained a promotion for war merit.

After 8 September 1943, when it was in Castrovillari with the 10th Group with the 84th with three MC 205s, the 90th with three MC 205s, the 91st Squadron with two MC 205s and the 9th Fighter Group at Gioia del Colle Airport with the 73rd with three MC 205s, the 96th with three MC 205s and the 97th Squadron with three MC 205s, the 4th Wing moved to Brindisi-Casale Airport and began collaborating with the Allied troops.

Lecce-Galatina Airport . In the first period of the "co-belligerence" it continued to use the fighters previously in service, the Macchi MC202 and MC205. Subsequently, it was re-equipped with 149 American aircraft, now very battered, of the Bell P-39N type, used only for the conversion of pilots, and P-39 Q, used in action.

The war actions, from September 1943 to April 1945, mainly concerned reconnaissance, strafing and attacks against German forces in the Balkans, where German defences and the unreliability of aircraft caused painful losses.
In the north, the 4th Wing, under the leadership of Fernando Malvezzi, gave birth to the 3rd "Francesco Baracca" Fighter Group of the National Republican Air Force.

73rd Squadron

The 73rd Fighter Squadron was a fighter unit of the Royal Army.

Verona-Tombetta Airfield of the III Group (later 3rd Land Fighter Group), in the change of names of all the squadrons on 15 April 1916, becomes the 73rd Squadron commanded by Captain Fernando Sanità who has four Aviatiks Salmson 140 hp in addition to the Lloyd C.II captured from the enemy.

- On 10 June 1940 he was in the 9th Fighter Group of the 4th Wing at Gorizia Airport with five Fiat CR.42s .

After Italy's entry into the war, the 9th Group was relocated from 20 June to Turin-Mirafiori Airport to participate in operations against France on the Western Front and moved on 29 June to Comiso Airport in Sicily to intervene on Malta and, subsequently, in North Africa.

From July 12th it arrives at Tripoli Airport with 19 pilots, including Lieutenant Reiner and Second Lieutenant Oblach , under the command of Lieutenant Pezzè , from 13 July at Berca Airport ; another pilot arrives at the end of the month and from 5 August at el-Adem T3 (then Gamal Air Base Abd el-Nasser). Following the British offensive, on 12 December the 9th Group moved to Martuba Airfield near Derna and the following day Oblach achieved his first individual victory.

While escorting five Savoia-Marchetti S.79 Sparviero bombers of the 60th Squadron of the 33rd Independent Land Bombing Group, which were attacking concentrations of enemy troops and armoured vehicles near Sollum , he engaged in combat with a formation of six Gloster fighters. Gladiator of No.3 RAAF Squadron shooting down one.

On the 19th, in another dogfight, Oblach damaged two Hawker fighters Hurricane .

The Wing returned to Italy at Christmas 1940 to switch to the Macchi MC 200s. In March 1941, as part of the Italian Campaign in Greece, it moved to Brindisi-Casale Airport with 12 MC 200s and for the Invasion of Yugoslavia from 4 April to Pola Airport with nine pilots commanded by Captain Mario Pluda .

In September of the same year, the Wing was transferred back to Sicily, returning to action once again in the skies of Malta.

On 17 October Oblach scored his second victory at the expense of a Bristol Blenheim bomber near Syracuse, while the following November he was at Comiso flying MC 202s.

After a short period of rest during the winter, it took part in a new operational cycle on Malta, which lasted until the beginning of the summer of 1942. Towards the end of May , the

4th Wing was transferred to North Africa to take part in the great Axis offensive led by General Erwin Rommel. From July 1942 the squadron passed to the command of Ten. Reiner , later promoted to Captain.

On October 9, 1942, Oblach shot down a Curtiss P-40 in the area of El Quteifiya , followed on the 20th of the same month by two P-40s in the Fuka area , and on the 25th another P-40. Oblach fell in combat on 1 December while carrying out an escort mission for some MC 200AS fighter-bombers engaged in a mission south-east of El Ahmar . After shooting down another P-40, his aircraft was in turn hit by another P-40 and crashed to the ground with the death of the pilot.

On 8 September 1943 he was in the IX Group at Gioia del Colle Airport with three MC 205s. On 2 May 1945 he was at Lecce-Galatina Airport in the 12th Fighter Group on P-39s of the 4th Fighter Wing.

Lieutenant Constantine Petrosellini

Costantino Petrosellini , born in 1921, was a second lieutenant reserve pilot when he was assigned to the 41st Squadron of the 63rd Group, based at Campoformido airport in Udine. Flying a Ro.37 biplane reconnaissance aircraft, he completed his first war missions against Yugoslavia; in July 1941 he began training on the Macchi MC 200 and was assigned to the 92nd Squadron of the 8th Group. During his career, he was decorated with three Silver Medals for military valor and a War Cross, as well as obtaining a promotion for war merits, shooting down 5 enemy aircraft, including a Flying Fortress. After the war he continued to fly in the Italian Air Force, entering the experimental department.

After leaving the Air Force he continued to fly in Alitalia as first Commander. He passed away in Rome on January 21, 2015.

Below is an extract from the diary of Lieutenant Costantino Petrosellini , a pilot of the Royal Air Force, for the period in which he fought in North Africa.

I arrived at the 8th fighter group, in Benghazi (airport K-3) at the beginning of May. It had been a transfer-transport of aircraft from Caselle (Turin). I was in command of a patrol of three Macchi MC 200s, which also included Pisano. The formation, of twelve airplanes, was under the command of the then captain Veronesi (known as "the Madonna of Loreto" for his ineffable qualities of character). I came from the 1941 operational cycle in Yugoslavia and, therefore, the difference in environment was immediately notable. In Benghazi, in May 1942, we had high-altitude cruise protection tasks over the port. Bacich had taken over command of the group a few days before, succeeding La Carruba.

The three squadrons were commanded by Zannier (92nd), Marcovich (93rd) and Cecchet (94th).

During one of the protection cruises over Benghazi, for reasons still unknown (perhaps a failure of the oxygen system), Second Lieutenant Franciosi crashed into the port . But the main purpose of that stop in Benghazi (after the brief advance from Agedabia) was to prepare the group for the next offensive that Rommel was preparing. The K-3 airfield was located on Balbia , just south of Benghazi.

The Macchi 200s were lined up under the trees to hide them from enemy observation. The general conditions were acceptable and we were starting to have our first experiences of radio communication. One day Serotini, who was on duty at the transmitter on the ground (on board we only had the receiver) told me (I was in cruise flight at a relatively low altitude):

"If you hear me, do a barrel roll," and I did. "If you hear me, turn left," and I turned.

Then he also told me "If you hear me, jump with the parachute" and I pretended not to hear...

On May 22, the three squadrons of the group moved to Martuba 5. Martuba was a location in the desert, about 50 km south of Derna : a desolate place, without a blade of grass, with the sun blazing, like in the movies. There were five airfields, populated by the 1st, 4th and 2nd (ours) Stormo, in addition to the Cr. 42s and Stukas of the 5th and 50th and the German Messerschmitts and Ju 88s.

All ready for the offensive.

As soon as we landed, in the morning, at Martuba 5, the dust had not even cleared when the English reconnaissance aircraft was already over our heads. And a few hours later, the bombers. It must have been three in the afternoon. A dozen Douglas Bostons showed up, escorted by a dozen P-40s. They dropped at random, but the 1st wing took off en masse and they were all shot down, except for one P-40. That night they made a reprisal bombing of the camps, just finished setting up.

The tents were still up for a bet and the English Wellingtons, one at a time, dropped flares and bombs all night long: it was driving us mad.

As I jumped , I found a hole (we hadn't had time to build shelters around the tents), I put myself in it, in the company of a dead Pole (I noticed it at dawn) dug up by hyenas.

The offensive proper began at dawn on 24 May 1942, when the 4th Wing attacked the entire British fighter force, Spitfires and P-40s, on the ground at Gambut airfield and almost completely destroyed it. The surprise was such that they found the planes still with the " hoods " on the engines.

The dominion of the sky was ours, so we began ground attacks in support of the ground troops that, from the line facing Ain el Gazala, began the advance to invest Tobruk .

They were terrible and beautiful days: in the midst of dust and sand, the formations took off, attacked the targets (tanks, convoys, enemy lines, stationary and moving), landed, refueled, set off again, and so on from dawn to dusk.

My followers were usually Moressi and Pisano, but I also often had Monti, Pavan and others with me. Zannier had left the command of the 92nd, which had been taken over by Sansone. This frenetic activity lasted practically a month, until the fall of Tobruk (June 21). It was a glorious period, woven with episodes of audacity and dedication that would take too long to enumerate.

All or nearly all of the aircraft returned from action damaged.

Some, unfortunately, did not return at all. We had very painful losses: Marcovich and Bottazzi , among others, were taken prisoner.

I commanded the formation that followed Cecchet 's .

Bottazzi 's plane catch fire and land without its landing gear in a cloud of dust and flames, while the anti-aircraft guns continued to fire at us like crazy. I really thought he hadn't made it out: instead, the English looked after him very well and with great humanity. On June 14, a squadron action (60 airplanes) against the lines and on the Balbla between EI Mrassas and Tobruk : we lost Sozzi and D'Agostini.

D'Agostini, just promoted to captain, had taken command of the 93rd, in place of Marcovich who had been taken prisoner: he landed safely with his undercarriage up, among the Australians who had gone mad after days and days of attacks from the sky. He was killed by gunshots (his body was found a few days later, when Tobruk had already fallen).

The gold medal was awarded in his memory.

But the living were no exception. Palumbo, with a calf full of splinters, immediately set off again for action, with blood dripping from him, and so did Pavan .

And all this while fighting against thirst, the heat, the sand, the blinding sun; and against the terrible anti-aircraft fire of the Tobruk fortress which was decimating us. Acroma , El Mrassas , Ain el Gazala, Mteifel he Ghebir , Southern Signals, Trlgh Capuzzo , Bir Hakeim , Tmimi are names we will never forget: they have remained in the soul and heart of us survivors like the hours of our lost youth (I was 21 years old at the time). We went to machine-gun low, "just above the sand", to look the enemy in the eye...

The Macchi 200 worked miracles, and we tried not to be inferior to it. As I said, Tobruk fell on June 21: 33,000 prisoners, 6,000 dead, full warehouses, food, petrol, vehicles, weapons and clothing in abundance. The entire 8th British Army practically destroyed.

On June 24th we moved to Ain el Gazala, on the English airport abandoned a few hours before. On June 29, with Moressi and Pisano, I moved to Derna to carry out the cruise of protection for the arrival of Mussolini who, as is known, then turned back without being able to enter Alexandria.

We stayed to catch our breath in Ain el Gazala. Sweet name: the source of gazelles; in fact, there was not a drop of water. A little peace, until July 5th.

That day, following the columns that were pressing the remnants of the 8th Army, we moved to Abu Haggag , close to the El Alamein lines. We landed in a terrible sandstorm and it was a coincidence that someone did not lose his life.

Qattara Depression loomed over us like the sword of destiny .

A Dantesque landscape, a steep ridge 300 metres high and underneath quicksand for a length of two or three hundred kilometres and a width of the same.

The air down there was unbreathable and the engines didn't want to "pull" when, flying low to the base of the ridge, we went to look for the English trucks. On the El Alamein line the English anti-aircraft had organized and we still had painful losses.

Casadio , of the 94th, threw himself with the whole plane against the lead armored car of an English column and exploded with it, stopping the entire column that was trying to bypass one of our strongholds. But the more the losses, the more tenacious, intense, intimate the friendship among the survivors became.

Other place names were added to the memory: Fuca , Bir Khalda , Qattara Spring , Salt Spring , Qattara Boring Works, Gebel Kalabin . The front stopped in El Alamein for a few months.

The war of position relegated us to escorting the convoys of motorboats that carried supplies along the coast, from Tobruk to Marsa. Matruh . It was a terrible job, because of the fatigue, the monotony, the climate: you can imagine what it meant to take off at one or two in the afternoon, from the Egyptian desert, and to make a two-hour cruise at 500 meters, at minimum speed on the motor rafts.

The plane was burning hot, literally: we were flying in shorts, bare-chested, with only life jackets and gloves to avoid burning our hands. Our logistics... worked as usual: no meat, fruit or fresh vegetables. Only biscuits and cans, so everyone was plagued by avitaminosis. And no mineral water, which, instead, was abundant in the rear.

The 92nd and 93rd (now commanded by Bissoli) remained at Abu Hag-gag , while the 94th had moved to Sidi he Barrani , which also served as a support camp for supplies.

It seemed like a dark job: but there were beautiful episodes. We often saved the motor-rocket from the sudden attacks of the " Beau fighters " , shooting down several of them. Lancia was also shot down, landed in the desert and returned to Abu Haggag , compass in hand, at night, on foot; and the sentries almost shot him.

At the end of September, Rommel attempted an offensive, which failed due to lack of fuel.

The Armoured Division Group was stuck behind the British lines, on the southern side of the El Alamein line. So on the night of 24 September the 8th Group, with isolated aircraft, was sent to machine-gun that area to hold the British (in particular two Indian divisions) while the Italian-Germans retreated to their starting positions with fuel obtained God knows how and rushed to the spot.

It was an epic, desperate action.

artificial horizons , nor any means of radio navigation. The on-board instruments had only a superficial illumination, and there was no means of defending oneself from the blinding flash of the machine guns when they fired.

No one had ever flown at night with the Macchi 200 (except poor Ruffini : only once!) and landing in the dark, in the desert, certainly did not present any particular safety features.

In short, we had no losses: and even today I cannot say whether it was luck or skill. A miracle, certainly, perhaps a combination of both. On October 15 we left Abu Haggag and retreated to Bu Amud , near Tobruk . The British offensive at El Alamein was close and easily predictable and it was vital to have a second line. Bu Amud had a fair amount of logistical equipment, drawn from what could be found at Tobruk , abandoned by the 8th Army in June.

We began to escort the incoming convoys, even at considerable distances from the coast, at the limit of autonomy. On October 26, I "caught", with Moressi and Pisano as wingmen, a "Maryland" at low altitude, just outside the port. It defended itself like a lion.

The fight moved to the piles above and I found myself alone with him. With a burst I hit him dead in the right engine.

He began to "flap his wings" in surrender, heading toward the coast. I fell into formation with him: it was then that the gunner from the turret aimed a burst at me at point-blank range that missed me by a hair. I fired again, until I saw him fall like a torch.

The retreat had taken a bad turn: on November 5 we were in Benghazi, back at K-3; Tobruk had been abandoned. We protected Benghazi as best we could from the English bombers.

We had several fights, but those already had the first " Liberators ". We moved to Nu fi lia , in the Gulf of Sirte, on November 15th and on the 21st to Marsa. he Aegia .

There we began to attack the English columns with wing bombs: the attacks had already been mounted at Abu Haggag by a team of armament technicians led by the then engineer captain Carlo Cao . We had mistreated them, we "pure hunters". But they, tough, had put the bomb attacks there anyway. And now they were coming good.

Every day the 8th group, now decimated in men and equipment, took off and dove down into the desert against the advancing

British armored forces. They were breathless actions: down from 5,000 meters, in a vertical dive, among the anti-aircraft guns that fired wildly, in the terrible furnace from which so many did not return.

And then, long-range flights into the desert to bring a greeting from above to our isolated and sacrificial garrisons. Moressi and I flew to Marada , a remote oasis in Sirte.

Almost eight hundred kilometers of desert there and back, beyond any imaginable autonomy of the Macchi 200.

Then landing with five minutes of gas: just enough to not break your neck just outside the airport.

And on December 1st the 8th group made its last action before repatriation. We managed to get a total of five Macchi 200s.

We loaded them with the two wing bombs and the machine gun belts and went off in the hellish heat. We turned out to sea and dived on the British positions towards Agheila .

Incredibly, the flak only opened up at the last moment and stopped immediately after we had got into a safe flight after the drop and strafing. In fact, twelve Spitfires swooped down on us. We were shorter and slower than them. We accepted the desperate fight. A Spitfire and two Macchi 200s crashed in flames. We could not find Monti; Calsolaro , seriously wounded, reached the coast by swimming. Sansone, Lancia and I returned disappointed, embittered, very sad for not having been able to do more, perhaps with the sense of guilt of not having sacrificed ourselves with the others.

On December 10, from Misurata, now overrun by the English and without any more aircraft, the survivors of the 8th fighter group returned to Catania with a formation of S.82s sent to recover them.

The facts and episodes that I have briefly described, the details that happened to me but that represent those of all the others, had as a common denominator the absolute sense of duty, the spirit of sacrifice without limits. Mario Bacich was always in the lead, in the riskiest actions, in the most tiring ones, in the moments of greatest commitment.

Each of us found in him, in his firmness of character (which sometimes revealed itself in explosive forms) the strength necessary to overcome sacrifices, bitterness, hardships, pains, regrets and fears.

Very human fears, at the sight of dearest friends dead: what if tomorrow it was my turn?

It was not my turn, because perhaps another fell in my place: these few lines, these tears that run down my face, are for you, my unknown pilot friend, who now flies forever, eternally young, in the purest sky of angels and heroes.

Lieutenant Constantine Petrosellini 8th Group Hunting